1

MW01490550

INVISIBLE CRIME

*Illegal Microchip Implants and
Microwave Technology
and Their Use Against Humanity*

by

Michael F. Bell

Brighton Publishing LLC
501 W. Ray Road
Suite 4
Chandler, AZ 85225
www.BrightonPublishing.com

The Invisible Crime

Illegal Microchip Implants and Microwave Technology and Their Use Against Humanity

by

Michael F. Bell

Brighton Publishing LLC

501 W. Ray Road
Suite 4
Chandler, AZ 85225
www.BrightonPublishing.com

First Edition

Printed in the United States of America

Copyright © 2011

ISBN 13: 978-1-936587-99-5

ISBN 10: 1-936-58799-8

Cover Design by Tom Rodriquez and Ted Schuyler

 # Dedication

This book is dedicated to heroes everywhere.

ᑫ A True Story ᕲ

Although this is a true story, certain names have been changed to protect both the innocent and the guilty.

"Do nothing in haste, look well to each step, and from the beginning think what may be the end."

~Edward Whymper, British climber and explorer known for the first ascent of the Matterhorn in 1865.

ᴄᴧᴼ Acknowledgements ᴏᴧᴐ

"The cruelest lies are often told in silence."
Robert Louis Stevenson

I would like to thank the people who offered assistance and support throughout the entire nightmare and living hell that became my life. Without the vast amount of in-depth information available from the Internet, the Beverly Hills Library, tips and general information from private investigators, other Targeted Individual Victims, declassified information and U.S. patents and documents, this book could not have been written.

I would also like to thank my friend, Sagitar and his family for helping me during my time of crisis in obtaining my first medical evidence in Madrid, Spain.

I wish to especially thank my mother and father, for allowing me to stay at their home in North Carolina, using their house as my bunker, seeking refuge during this most disturbing time, protecting myself from this bizarre, seemingly endless and ongoing crime. I am quite literally like a man without a country, nowhere to run, no place to hide.

ᑫᔆ Preface ᕮᔌ

"Behold ye scoffers, For I will work wonders in your days, which ye will not believe."
Book of Rabakkuk

In this account, I refer to the Targeted Individual as the Target or the Victim.

What if someone could read your mind, manipulate your dreams, and see and hear everything that you do? What if you were followed and tracked everywhere you went? What if voices were electronically beamed into your head and you were shocked by directed or microwave energy, just as you were drifting off to sleep? What if the technology that made this all possible had actually been in existence for over fifty years and kept secret? What if you became the Victim of this crime and technology and nobody believed you?

What would you do?

It's not science fiction; it's called "psychotronic weaponry" and it uses the current existing satellite and cellular phone system. It is the result of combining the two words, psychological and

4

electronic. Perpetrators using this technology torture and murder thousands of American citizens and people around the world, most never knowing what happened. This crime leaves little or no evidence.

Recently declassified, this technology is also known as non-lethal weaponry, although it can cause instant-staged heart attacks and automobile accidents, strokes, and severe and debilitating mental disorders. The constant, continuous low-level exposure of electromagnetic or microwave energy can cause cancer and tumors that can lead to a long, slow, painful death.

Surprisingly, this technology is legal and available for purchase by anyone on the Internet. It's sold under the guise of "experimental or entertainment purposes only; should not be misused." The manufacturer or distributor is legally bound to include a small clause within the instructions for use that "eliminates the seller of any responsibility of misuse, intentional, or accidental." This clause relinquishes the seller of all responsibility.

This technology can also incorporate the use of injected, inserted, or surgically installed microchip or biochip implants. Once implanted in an unwitting Victim, these devices can be used to monitor, spy on, GPS track, torture, or kill the Victim remotely. Sometimes this electronic harassment or electronic stalking can be performed from thousands of miles away from the Victim, via satellite and cellular network systems.

The modern day version of this system has the capability to

read a person's mind in real time and give the Victim the notion to do something, as if by command. Because this notion is perceived by the Victim in the first person, the Victim perceives this idea or way of thinking as a product of his own thought process. People that become the Target of conditional mind control will be unable to discern and distinguish their own thoughts from those that are being projected to them.

Every human being has a signature brain wave electroencephalogram (EEG) that is unique and different from any other person's brain wave pattern. In this respect, the EEG can be compared to a fingerprint. An alternative method of mind control involves a process which captures a person's unique brain wave pattern and locks onto it using the GPS satellite system. Once this brain wave frequency is grabbed by a computer, that person can be tracked anywhere in the world in real time. This system represents the most refined part of electronic stalking.

A person's thoughts can be read and manipulated in the same way as that of a biochip implant, without having a device covertly placed in their body. If removed, a microchip implant makes the Targeted Individual's claims credible and legitimate.

The EEG, a signature brain wave method of mind control, is basically impossible to detect and use to prove that the person is a Victim of any crime.

The most difficult aspect of being a Victim of this crime is convincing other people—in particular law enforcement—that the person is being victimized. The very concept that someone would follow another person, make small, but noticeable damage to personal property, and constantly, subtly harass the Victim, for no reason, sounds absurd.

These crimes are so bizarre and so illogical sounding that speaking of it cannot help but make the Victim appear paranoid, delusional, schizophrenic, or suffering from dementia.

The Perpetrators count on the fact that nobody will believe the Victims, completely discrediting them. This makes organized stalking, electronic harassment, and mind control perfect crimes.

Mind control was crudely conceived and first developed during the Korean War. It was based on three basic principles: 1) sleep deprivation, 2) solitary confinement, and 3) relentless interrogation sessions. Through these extreme methods, the human mind could be changed and its basic "hard drive" altered, permanently.

Mind control can also be traced back to World War II as part of the Nazi Human Behavior and Experimentation Program. Here, Hitler and the Nazi regime, took the Chinese form of mind control one step further. This program was captured by the U.S. Military at the end of the war. German scientists were then offered to work for the United States before this information was intercepted by Russia and the rest of the world. Known as "Operation Paperclip," now an even more advanced and further refined program would be developed by the United States government within classified top secret military operations.

This program was first introduced to the C.I.A. in the 1950s and officially continued through the mid-1970s, known as Project MK-ULTRA. The "MK" stands for Mind Kontrol. "ULTRA" describes "breaking the code." So, literally, this represents the breaking or conditioning of the human mind.

This program was covert, illegal human experimentation. Through a variety of techniques using drugs and various forms of human behavior modification, the C.I.A. could not only put thoughts into the mind and create false memories, but also had the ability to erase specific memories and make the individual forget a certain event or even permanently change basic thought patterns.

LSD-25 was one of many drugs used on subjects in these illegal experiments. These techniques were used on unwitting subjects, American citizens, from every race, age, social and economic status, and even on its own military.

Although Chloroform and Ether are now considered "old school drugs" by criminal organizations like the Mafia, they are still used to this day in abduction and kidnapping cases.

Scopolamine or Devils' Breath—also known as Hyoscine—is derived from the native Columbian Burundanga Tree, part of the nightshade classification of plants. It's now recognized as the world's most dangerous drug and is used in a large percentage of abduction cases worldwide.

Rohypnol, the famed date rape drug, is another popular choice for criminals for abduction, rape, and robbery. The above mentioned drugs are usually colorless, odorless, and tasteless. Because of the great strength of these drugs, very little of the poison is necessary to drug someone and achieve the desired result of amnesia. When surreptitiously mixed into food or a beverage, it's nearly impossible for the Victim to be aware that they are being drugged.

Through the direct connection to the human optic nerve, retinal implants and EEG technology allows the controller or operator to actually see through the Victim's eyes. Using the Victim's eyes as their cameras, Perpetrators are able to see all the Victim sees. This same electronic connection to the ear canals using illegal, covert cochlear ear implants and the human auditory system enables the controller to hear what the Victim hears, as well as what he says—all in real time.

If this information were to leak into the hands of terrorists or criminals, the potential for catastrophic disaster is unthinkable.

That is exactly what has happened, not only in America, but globally. The U.S. Government denies the existence of this unconscionable weaponry and it is embarrassed, ashamed, and reluctant to admit that it has lost control of its own technology to organized crime and hate groups around the world.

This crime has become the world's dirtiest little secret.

To compound the thought-reading and thought-inserting capabilities of implants or EEG technology, organized stalking or gang stalking, combined with electronic harassment, can make the Victim's life unbearable. By ganging-up on or bullying a Target continuously, the Target's life becomes a nightmare of terror and psychological harassment.

The Invisible Crime - Michael F. Bell

Isolation is the goal: to strip the person of all privacy and humiliate, mock, and taunt the Victim over and over. It drives many Victims to commit suicide. This organized, covert crime is carried out by sociopaths or psychopathic individuals who have no conscience. They are well-funded, highly organized, and they use all the latest technology to constantly refine, update, and revolutionize this most perfect crime.

At this point, before this isolated incident and story is presented, it is important for any Targeted Individuals reading this to know that their situation will never change, unless they make the efforts necessary to change things themselves. Very quickly, the Victims realize that no one is going to suddenly appear to rescue them.

In this book, I offer practical advice on how to be proactive. I offer countermeasure techniques and methods to help Targeted Individuals regain their health and happiness and to take back their lives. If the Targeted Individual chooses to do nothing, the harassment will most likely never go away and usually lasts for life.

At the very beginning of this story, I want the reader to know I am not schizophrenic, paranoid, or delusional. I do not suffer from dementia or any form of mental illness.

I could never figure out how the people who were stalking and harassing me always knew where I was going or what I was doing. After taking my apartment apart piece by piece, searching for covert cameras, microphones, and searching my entire vehicle for a GPS tracker, I finally realized that *I was the tracking device.*

The intent of this book is to expose this heinous, covert crime and make the general public aware of these devices and weapons and ultimately make amendments to the U.S. Constitution and the Patriot Act, to outlaw this technology completely and its use on human beings.

This crime is nothing short of diabolical. All covert technology and devices mentioned in this book are real. Mind control and Operation MK-ULTRA have been used and kept secret since the Second World War. V2K—or voice-to-skull technology—has been in existence since 1974. The Target becomes a real life voodoo doll at the mercy of the criminals.

This technology is used on its Victims without their knowledge or consent, and in and of itself, is one of the most evil things man has done to mankind.

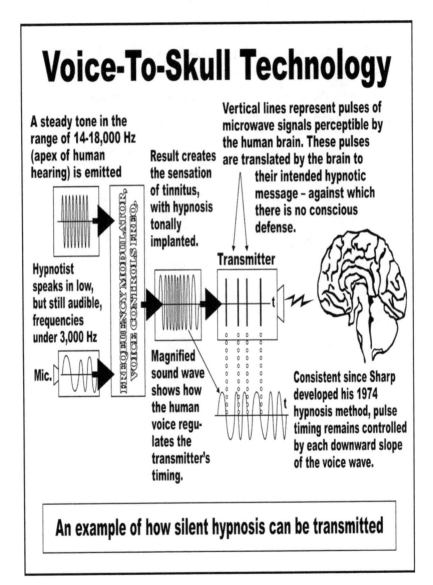

Voice-To-Skull Technology

A steady tone in the range of 14-18,000 Hz (apex of human hearing) is emitted

Result creates the sensation of tinnitus, with hypnosis tonally implanted.

Vertical lines represent pulses of microwave signals perceptible by the human brain. These pulses are translated by the brain to their intended hypnotic message – against which there is no conscious defense.

Hypnotist speaks in low, but still audible, frequencies under 3,000 Hz

Mic.

FREQUENCY MODULATOR, VOICE CONTROLS FREQ.

Transmitter

t

Magnified sound wave shows how the human voice regulates the transmitter's timing.

Consistent since Sharp developed his 1974 hypnosis method, pulse timing remains controlled by each downward slope of the voice wave.

An example of how silent hypnosis can be transmitted

12

⇜ Chapter One ⇝

How It All Started: A Brief Background

"Oh Lord, if there is a Lord, save my soul, if I have a soul..."
Joseph Ernst Renan

My name is Michael Fitzhugh Bell. I was born on October 27, 1961 in Greenwich, Connecticut. I am the oldest of three children, with two younger sisters.

In retrospect, I was different from other children in many ways. I am left-handed when writing and using a utensil such as a fork; in sports, I'm ambidextrous. I have a photographic memory and a strong intuition or sixth sense about people, places, things, and events. I was also fortunate enough to have been born with what others consider to be a good sense of humor. I also possess a vivid, creative imagination. These inherent qualities are part of my life and who I am. Although I would never discuss these gifts with others, people would often notice them and make me aware of my own personality. I didn't know it then, but these gifts would come to help me later in life and assist other people close to me.

I went to boarding school or prep school in New England at the age of twelve. I attended Eaglebrook School in Deerfield, Massachusetts and Brooks School in North Andover, Massachusetts. I attended two colleges: Eckerd College in St. Petersburg, Florida and Occidental College in Eagle Rock, California. To be honest, I never really enjoyed school or the college curriculum, except for English and writing. Writing was the only area where I felt comfortable expressing my ideas, views, and imagination.

I was a typical American teenager growing up, interested in sports—mainly soccer and ice hockey. Like my grandfather and father before me, I was a New York Rangers hockey fan, always hoping for that elusive Stanley Cup. This dream was later realized for me and other Rangers fans with a Stanley Cup win in 1994, the first Championship win for the New York Rangers in fifty-three years.

I left Occidental after the beginning of my senior year. I returned to my hometown and bounced around Greenwich, Connecticut taking low-end jobs such as mail clerk at a market research firm and office gopher at a prestigious local law firm.

I was a directionless dreamer who lived by himself in a small apartment in town. I had a natural ability to cook and create and decided to apply for a position in the kitchen of a famous yacht club in Greenwich. In cooking, I found something in which I could excel while still being challenged, which led to a great sense of accomplishment. Over a five-year period, I cooked at several different local country clubs that provided free room and board. In those days, I would party my money away, never saving for the future, living in the moment. This lifestyle caused a degree of shame and embarrassments for my family, who had hoped that I would become focused and make something of myself, like so many of their friends' children.

I attended the Culinary Institute of America in Hyde Park, New York, and graduated with honors in 1992.

In 1994, my sister married a famous America's Cup skipper, a living legend in the world of sailing. He offered me a job as a cook for his sailing team in the 1995 America's Cup Campaign in San Diego, California. That job lasted nine months from beginning to end.

After the America's Cup, I chose to stay and live in California, working at high-end restaurants and hotels in the kitchen position of Garde Manager, Chef de Partie, or Roundsman in San Diego, Coronado, Point Loma, and LaJolla, California.

After a weekend outing with a girlfriend in Palm Springs, California, I became enchanted with the desert's beauty and serenity. Palm Springs, for those who have not been there, is a town nestled at the base of Mount San Jacinto, a nearly 11,000 foot mountain. Upon seeing it for the first time, I was blown away by its idyllic setting. I decided to move there. I became interested in mountain climbing and climbed Mount San Jacinto and other neighboring mountains. I would often spend an entire day exploring and hiking in either Taquitz or Palm Canyons, both within walking distance of my apartment.

After seeing *Good Will Hunting*, I became inspired to write again, and I wanted to write a screenplay of my own. I entered my first screenplay, entitled *The Devil's Canyon,* in Matt Damon and Ben Affleck's first screenwriting contest in 2001—Project Greenlight. Out of nearly twenty-thousand applicants, my screenplay advanced as a finalist. Although I did not win the contest, it was a great, positive reinforcement for my writing. I knew I was on the right track.

It was also at this time I began writing articles for Palm Springs Life Magazine. This was my first official published writing. Thanks to then chief editor Stewart Weiner, I got my big break to write and become a *published* author.

❧ Chapter Two ❧

Creating a Slave

"For the thing I greatly feared has come upon me. And what I dreaded has happened to me. I am not at ease, nor am I quiet; I have no rest, for trouble comes."
Job 3:25, 26

After five years of writing and working as a chef in Palm Springs and Palm Desert, California, I knew if I wanted to sell any of my work, I would have to live closer to the source—Hollywood, just a two hour drive from my Palm Springs apartment.

In 2001, I moved to a tiny, sparse, single apartment building on Chula Vista Way in Hollywood, California. It had barely enough room to hold all my belongings and furniture. The good thing was that this apartment was in a great location and only cost $500 per month.

After just two weeks of living there, a former catering/cooking friend offered me a job cooking on Mark

Burnett's reality show, *Combat Missions*. Principle filming only lasted six weeks, but it put me in touch with other motion picture caterers in and around the Hollywood area. Chefs can make as much as six to seven hundred dollars a day working on a TV series or motion picture doing location catering, but they are usually sixteen-hour days, six days a week, cooking on a truck in a mobile kitchen, and with a great deal of pressure and stress. Taking home an average of $2,000 per week and traveling around the country cooking for movie casts, crews, and talent was not only exciting, but monetarily rewarding.

Between working as a chef on-site for movies, commercials, and TV series, I would get a chance to do my screenwriting. For a new writer, selling a script in Hollywood is like selling sand at the beach. It's hard to find an agency willing to read an unsolicited, submitted query letter—let alone a script.

In 2003, I was driving on Sunset Boulevard, returning to my apartment from a Starbucks coffee run, when I was rear-ended by a tow truck carrying another vehicle, severely injuring my neck, back, and left knee. This was the beginning of a dark pattern of events that would come to haunt and ruin my life. It was also on that same day that I met a neighbor who lived across the street from my apartment building. This fateful meeting would later become a moment of great regret.

Brian Eastfall was a twenty-seven-year-old hippie artist who dressed in black, homemade clothing. He sported long dreadlocks and had several distinct, dark tattoos and symbols on his arms. He had permanent paint and stains on his hands which seemed to be from constant drawing and painting spills and exposure to charcoal and colored pencils. He was unemployed and lived with his thirty-seven-year-old Japanese girlfriend, Kimza. She was quiet, attractive, and seemingly the opposite of her boyfriend.

I remember Brian proudly showing me his artwork, a collection of primitive drawings, sketches, and paintings, each with some kind of demonic undertone. He had created a website on which he would sell his artwork for unusually high prices. Most of his subject matter consisted of strange creatures. Black was the dominant color, with only the minimum of bright colors used. If a psychologist were to try to interpret this art as classic Rorschach ink-blot images, he could only draw one logical conclusion: that the artist was deeply depressed, delusional, angry, and psychotic.

When Brian asked me what I thought of his creations, I answered, unsure, "Wow, that's…really unique."

This day would later become a day of remorse, for soon afterwards, a string of bad luck and harassment began. A new tenant moved into the apartment below mine and would stay up all night, partying, and playing loud music. Every night was a party with a new group of friends. It was the beginning of what would be described as a *noise campaign*. The once quiet neighborhood and apartment building soon became increasingly loud and disruptive during my usual serene morning-writing time.

Every night, just as I was going to sleep, I would hear slamming doors, banging, and hammering on walls. Continuous flushing of toilets in adjacent apartments and the sound of running water in the next door sink or bathtub awakened me and left me sleep deprived and stressed. The intermittent honking of horns from the garage beneath my building, firecrackers exploding in the middle of the night, yelling and loud laughter, and constant foot traffic of tenants coming and going made this once-perfect writer's pad into an ongoing den of noise, and endless frustration. Even after repeated complaints to the building's management and many police reports filed concerning the tenant living directly below me, the noise campaign continued.

At this time, I also noticed that my pride and joy—a small, black Mercedes-Benz C230 Kompressor sports car—was constantly being vandalized. I tried to keep the car perfect, but I would notice small scratches appearing in places that only I would notice. The driver's door handle was scratched, a small key-job was evident on the door, and a huge scratch suddenly appeared by the gas cap. Living in a big city like Los Angeles with all the traffic and tight parking, it's hard to keep a car from getting tarnished; but when small damage becomes noticeable on a daily basis it didn't take long to figure out that this damage was no accident or coincidence.

I also noticed damage inside my apartment, such as gouges in the walls, stains, and scratches on the kitchen floor where there hadn't been any before. The venetian blinds covering my porch and sliding door leading out to the small balcony were always getting broken and left on the floor. Small things like coasters on tables and even pieces of furniture were moved to other areas around my apartment.

I suspected that someone was getting into my apartment while I was out. When I informed the property manager about my suspicions, he would look at me in disbelief and say that it just did not sound possible.

Months later, after finally convincing him that I was telling the truth, it was the manager of my particular building who came to bat for me. He stuck up for me and confided in me what other tenants in the building were saying about me behind my back. Evidently, a malicious rumor campaign had been started, saying things about me that weren't true. Those things included: I was a criminal, or that I was gay, or a pedophile—or —I was a spy trying to undermine the United States government. I was shocked and angry to have anything untrue said about me—especially behind my back.

When I was out of town and working on a movie, I would return to my apartment to find lights I had left turned on earlier, were later turned off—and closet doors were open, when I had left them closed. I also noticed small chips in china plates and cracked glasses, especially with my photographic memory. I could clearly see things were different and that someone was getting into my apartment and leaving behind small, but obvious, evidence of illegal entry.

After months of continuous noise harassment, impeding my ability to write—and more importantly causing severe sleep deprivation—there were also odd electronic disturbances, such as flickering and browning of my lights at night. My computer would often turn off by itself. I decided to move.

My parents had visited once in the five years I lived in that apartment and they could not understand how anyone could live in such a small place. Clearly, I could afford to live somewhere much nicer.

I also traded in my car and got a brand new, black Mercedes-Benz E350. I would spend hours washing, polishing, and maintaining its clean and perfect appearance, and then stand back and admire it. It was the only luxury in my life.

As an aspiring screenwriter determined to sell a script in the movie capital of the world, I decided to stay in Los Angeles, and moved across town to a beautiful apartment on the prestigious row of upscale housing on Burton Way.

Two weeks after I moved in with all new furniture, the noise campaign began again and small damage to my car and scratches on the newly painted white walls began appearing. New sheets were ripped. Holes and puncture marks showed up on my brand new pillow cases. Upon closer inspection, I found small dents and nicks in the brand new paint on my car. Sometimes, even when the car sat for days or weeks without being used, it would end up with flat tires and deep scratches in the alloy wheels, which would upset me to no end. As soon as I had this damage repaired, similar damage would happen to another wheel.

It was also at this time, that I noticed a Japanese tenant living down the hall from me would mysteriously leave his apartment at exactly the same time I left mine. At first I thought it was just a strange coincidence, but my neighbor would exit his apartment just as I was locking my door behind me—every day, even if I changed my schedule. As we walked down the hall together towards the stairs, I would say, "Good morning." He would never reply—instead, he would give me a hard, angry stare. After a while, I gave up saying hello to this jerk and walked down the hall ahead of him and down the stairs by myself.

Random cars would park outside my apartment in the alley behind the building and the drivers would just sit there chatting loudly on their cellphones or blast the music on their stereos. These cars always had their high-beam headlights on, even in the middle of the day.

My father had sent me a cellphone jammer for fun and entertainment purposes only. With this device, I could block the cellphone conversation of anyone within one hundred feet of my apartment, through walls and closed windows. I could now instantly end an unwanted, intrusive, nearby conversation. I had to stop using this device covertly and all together, because now the use of a cellphone blocker is against the law in California.

As soon as my one-year lease was up, I wanted to move again. In addition to all the regular continuous noises associated with living in an urban environment and the continuous noise campaign, there was also a city bus depot across the street from my apartment. The thunderous sounds and deep rumbling and vibrations of the buses coming and going were inescapable—even with earplugs.

The Invisible Crime - Michael F. Bell

I moved again in spring of 2007 to another apartment building half-a-mile away on the Beverly Hills borderline, in a quieter, slightly less-trafficked area. The first month was a dream: I had plenty of good writing time, lots of quiet, my environments was stress-free, and I got excellent, much-needed sleep.

As if on cue, the familiar disruptive noises and property damage began appearing. This time, my clothing—most of it brand new—started to show signs of wear and tear in exactly the same places. The right armpits and sides of all my shirts were ripped, and all had big holes beneath the bottom front button. All of my shorts and blue jeans had small holes in the crotch, in places where no one would feel comfortable having an opening.

An air conditioner in the apartment above mine was partially broken and would make a deep hum and vibrate throughout each night, making it impossible to sleep. Despite appealing to management to fix the air conditioner, it remained unrepaired.

I started to feel nauseous and began getting terrible headaches. From somewhere, a gas or some chemical with a distinct acidic smell would permeate throughout my apartment. I finally traced this leakage to the drains in the bathroom sink and shower/tub drains. A terrible, strong sulfur stench would also fill the air in my apartment during the day.

Other things were occurring to make me feel as if I had lost my mind. A full bottle of shampoo would be empty the next day except for one small drop. The same thing would happen to a new tube of toothpaste. Full jars of vitamins would have only one vitamin left in them. Not only was this occurrence frustrating, it became expensive to replace empty bottles of body lotion or bars of soap every few days. Whenever I opened a new product, I would have to mark the date down on the calendar to prove to myself that it was not just my imagination that they were being used up so quickly.

Afraid of being called crazy for reporting this ongoing strange set of coincidence patterns, I decided to investigate on the Internet. I began searching things like "moved furniture," "property damage," "vehicle damage," and "constant noise patterns." Two phrases kept appearing: "organized stalking" and "gang stalking."

I had never heard of such a crime, but all of the information on the websites I visited described in detail exactly the same weird things that were happening to me—including the strange smells, slamming doors, and loud music. There were other things mentioned which I did not notice before—things such as garbage left in front of my door and finding my apartment door open when I knew I had locked it when I left. Now all these things that I had read about were happening to me—but why?

I had never attended the art shows held by my old neighborhood acquaintance, Brian, although he always would send me an email invitation. However, in late September of 2007, I decided to get away from the "cursed and seemingly haunted apartment" and attend one of his shows.

The Invisible Crime · Michael F. Bell

Brian and his Japanese girlfriend, Kimza, greeted me when I arrived at 7:00 p.m. I immediately noticed that everyone there— except for me, Brian, and some of his friends that perform together in an alternative music band—was Japanese. Brian speaks and writes Japanese fluently. Other than Kimza, I didn't know any Japanese people.

Nothing unusual took place at this event. I stuck around for about three hours. I had taken a taxi cab to this art show, in the event I had any wine or beer, I didn't want to drive home. Brian and Kimza quickly volunteered to drive me back home. They dropped me off outside my latest apartment complex. Before this particular night, I hadn't disclosed to them my new address.

Three months later, I sat in an apartment alone and became increasingly aware something was wrong with this situation. My neighbors and other tenants would leave the building whenever I exited. These same people would magically appear just as I returned to the building. It is a technique known as *enter/exit*, a stalking method designed to annoy and confuse the Targeted Individual: me. This method, over time, will make the Victims paranoid and appear delusional should they try to explain it to another person.

The more I read about organized stalking by proxy, the more aware and sensitized I became to my situation. I had read about being potentially drugged, and I became very proactive. Drugging the Victims or poisoning them were other popular tactics used by Perpetrators. No longer could I risk leaving half-finished food or open containers in the refrigerator. I had to *one-time*

26

everything. That means I would have to buy prepared food and consume it all at one time, one meal at a time. Anything left over would have to be thrown out to avoid drugging potential.

I discovered and suffered all of this by myself because there was no one to whom I could explain this bizarre crime. Who would believe me? It was just too strange.

Out of nowhere, I started to get terrible headaches and stomach aches. Normally, I was unusually healthy, with few or no physical complaints. Even the pain from my car accident, three years earlier, had diminished to a point where it was not bothering me.

I had read that a popular tactic used by Perpetrators is to dismantle a microwave in the Victim's apartment, then reassemble it so that it functions and now leaks deadly microwave energy. Without spending money on a microwave leak detector, here is an easy and effective method for testing any microwave oven for leakage. While the oven is off, place a cellphone inside and shut the door. *Do not* turn the oven on. Then, either using a hardline phone or another cellphone, try to call the one that is inside the microwave oven. If the cellphone inside the oven does not ring, that means the microwave is sealed properly. If the cellphone does ring, either repair or replace the microwave oven.

Starting on January 1, 2008, I began feeling very weird. I had a terrible fear in the pit of my stomach, and my eyesight and vision had changed. As I sat at my desk writing, the periphery of my vision was distorted. Out of the corner of my eye, I would perceive a fixed object—like a lamp—move slightly, and then return to its original position. My eyes became very sensitive to sunlight.

I had been drugged with LSD-25. Drugging individuals with this substance is accomplished by putting it in their toothpaste, shampoo, hand lotion, or any toiletries. This drug can be applied to a door handle or directly on a toothbrush, and can be absorbed into the system via these covert methods. Even items such as toilet paper or tissue paper, pillows, and sheets can all be tainted with drugs. So what I couldn't wash or clean, I threw out.

Because I was unable to determine the exact source of my drugging, whenever I left my apartment, I had to bring all of my toiletries and open containers with me in a small backpack. That way, I knew for sure that these items were still pristine and untainted. I also had to go through other precautionary steps like constantly using products like Windex to wipe down all doorknobs and cabinet doorknobs. Nothing was out of the realm of possibility. Even things like clean silverware and utensils had to be washed again before using them.

I even went to an optometrist to see if there was something wrong with my vision just to eliminate that possibility. My eye exam was normal. When I went to my regular doctor complaining about headaches and occasional nausea, he simply said that it was most likely a flu or a cold, as it was cold season that time of the year.

One night, I decided to watch some cable TV and have a

beer. After one sip of beer, I felt immediately tired and fell asleep on top of my bed still fully dressed. I didn't know it at the time, but I had been drugged with a powerful drug and hallucinogen called Scopolamine. Even though the bottle of beer I was drinking from was unopened, the top end of the bottle, from which I drank, was evidently *painted* with this drug.

Victims of most date rape drugs will be able to recall what happened to them under hypnosis. This is not possible with Scopolamine, because the memory is completely blocked and never formed. Therefore, it's nearly impossible to have a Victim remember, that which was never recorded by the brain's formation of a particular memory.

I woke up in what at first I thought was a dream. I was being escorted down a long underground tunnel or hallway to a room at the end. My vision was cloudy and blurry, and I was hallucinating both in my hearing and my vision. I felt like I was slightly drunk, but I had only taken one sip of the beer before going to sleep.

In my dream, two individuals dressed in long, black robes and wearing strange, full-face masks held me on either side by my arms. They were silently walking and guiding me closer to the room at the end of the hall. The room was dimly lit by amber colored candles that cast eerie shadows upon the walls.

Approximately twelve to fifteen people, all wearing the same kind of black robes and carnival masks, sat Indian-style in a circle. The carnival masks were held in place by an elastic band.

They only covered part of the person's face—the area surrounding the eyes and part of the nose. Although all of these people wore masks, it was still easy for me to see that these people were Asian; enough of their facial features were visible to make this distinction. However, I noticed the exception was that one masked man was not Asian; and his face was somewhat familiar. Then, I noticed something I will never forget: a familiar tattoo on the top of his left hand—it was Brian.

I was led to the middle of the circle and gestured to sit down. In the background, there were the awful sounds of people screaming and crying.

Scopolamine is often used in abduction cases especially in its homeland of Columbia in South America. The unwitting Victim of a small dose of this powerful drug will act and speak normally, without any trace of being intoxicated, but they will remember little or none of their experience.

Fifty percent of all Targeted Individuals or abduction Victims that are drugged with Scopolamine die. Proper weight and size ratios must be calculated perfectly for the Victim to survive. The effects of Scopolamine do not last long, and the person being drugged develops a quick tolerance to the drug's effects. Therefore, to keep a Victim under its influence, they must be constantly re-drugged, approximately every eight to twelve hours, with an ever-increasing, higher dosage to achieve the same effect.

This is the world's most dangerous drug. Burundanga or Boracherra, as it is known in Columbia, loosely translates to "get you drunk." It's a favorite drug in the criminal underworld and very accessible. It's as easy to obtain as Heroin or Cocaine; but, there is nothing recreational about Scopolamine. It has only criminal elements to it, mostly for abduction, sex, and/or robbery. The Victim suffers nearly complete amnesia, and is only barely able to remember the few moments between druggings. This was where my gifts had helped me; my intuition and my photographic memory—although challenged—prevailed.

I remember while sitting in the center of the circle of people wearing strange masks, looking at who I knew was my neighbor, Brian. I spoke out loud, "Dude, why are you letting this happen to me?" There was no answer.

The leader, sitting at one side of the circle, was the only person who spoke. I looked at him; his face appeared slightly blurred and seemingly half melted. He looked at me and said, "Michael, do you know what is going to happen tonight?"

I looked at him and replied, "No."

He said that his name was "Queenie"—and he told me matter-of-factly, "Tonight, you are going to die."

On top of being held in the vice-like grip of this terrible drug, and being in a strange and scary place, the thought of being killed was overwhelming. I started to cry and asked, "What? Why? No, no, no, why?"

The Invisible Crime - Michael F. Bell

The leader looked long and hard at me, examining how this terrible news had affected me. He asked, "Do you have anything you would like to say—before you leave this world?"

I started talking, going on and on as if I were in some sort of filibuster, thinking perhaps if I talked long enough or said the right thing, maybe I could make them change their minds.

There was a stone altar located directly behind the leader with a lit candle sitting in the center of it. I thought to myself, *Nobody knows I'm down here. Now they are going to sacrifice me to the Devil, and when they're done with me, they'll take my body and bury it out in the desert, and that will be the end of me.* I also remember thinking at this point, as horrible as it was that I would die, no one would ever see me again. I would just disappear, and my poor family would never know the truth. They would know, most likely, that something very bad had happened to me—but, I would just be lost…forever.

There was just enough movement in the air to make the candle flicker, and on the wall behind the altar, I began to see hallucinations. The shadows looked like a fierce and angry dragon. The shadows kept changing and switching the way the image appeared, making it look alive and then making it disappear. From somewhere, I could still hear the lonely, pitiful screams of agony and despair.

Despite being in this situation, my intuition took over. I could see these were simply people hiding behind strange looking masks.

The Invisible Crime - Michael F. Bell

My heart was racing, and I was sweating profusely. I knew that they had given me some kind of powerful drug, and I knew if I kept talking and telling stories about my life, at least I was still alive. I talked about a favorite dog my family had when I was growing up—Lilly White, and how much I loved her. I talked about my travels, my favorite TV shows, and how I really enjoyed the music from certain sitcoms. It was like I was being given my Last Rites. Nobody stopped me from talking, so I kept on, hoping to keep my life a little longer.

At one point, the drug overpowered me and I collapsed backwards, feeling very drowsy, onto the stone floor. Then, everything went black.

The next thing I can remember is lying on a flat, cold, stainless steel table, in a small, dark room with no windows. There were two men standing over me wearing white surgical masks, light green surgeon's shirts, and had latex gloves on their hands. There was a very bright light shining directly into my eyes. I could barely see and had to squint. Light sensitivity is one of many side effects of the drug, Scopolamine. I could hear instruments sliding and being moved on a small table next to one of the masked men standing over me.

I was so frightened, I could not even speak. Out of the corner of my eye, another man held a syringe. I distinctly remember this because it was a real medical syringe with a stainless steel handle and a finger-loop which I knew was used for pressing down on the lever to release the contents inside.

The man standing over me looked at the other man and silently nodded.

Then, I was sent into blackness with one last memory. Fully anesthetized, I fell into a deep sleep.

ᴄᴐ Chapter Three ᴇᴑ

Something Is Horribly, Terribly Wrong
"Truth is stranger than fiction, but it is because fiction is obligated to stick to possibilities; truth isn't."
Mark Twain

I woke up in a strange room, much like a guest room in a very nice house. I lay on a large bed with nice sheets, blankets, and a pillow. Some of my clothing was still on me, including my pants and boxer shorts, but my shirt was off and my shoes and socks were on the floor. A pile of assorted coats and jackets was stacked on a chair on one side of the room. I was in an extra room that had been used as a coat room, in the way people do for their guests at dinner parties.

I remember very well seeing a digital clock on a nearby table with red numerals; it read 1:33 p.m. I looked around the room, and saw one window behind me. It was a bright, sunny day outside. In the background, I could see hills and houses on these hills. It seemed as if I was on the second floor of the house, as I had a commanding view looking down on a small lawn and a

35

lovely garden below the window.

The Scopolamine was wearing off at this point, and I remember how bright the sun was. I still had to squint, as this bright light hurt my eyes. I could see a very nice mansion next door with tall palm trees and beautiful landscaping surrounding it.

This is one of my strongest memories during this abduction. Even now, I can remember thinking that it was a large mansion in the Beverly Hills or Bel Air area. The hills in the background looked familiar. I had seen them from another angle while hiking in Runyon Canyon and in Bronson Park, looking down on these hills from my favorite hike up above the famed Hollywood Sign.

The effects of the Scopolamine were diminishing to the point that I was able to get dressed, so I put on my shirt, socks, and shoes. I stood up and felt a little dizzy.

Although my vision was slightly blurry, I could see a single door across the room. I knew I had to try to escape from this terrible nightmare, get outside, and try to get back to my apartment somehow so I could tell someone what had happened to me.

As I approached the door, what looked like two decorative knights standing on either side of the door wearing black robes, suddenly came to life, and blocked the door. They were two sentry guards that had been standing perfectly still, wearing masks, left to watch me. They silently stood between me and the door; I knew it was hopeless and went back and sat on the edge of the bed.

I was so disoriented from the Scopolamine; I had not even

noticed that they were there until they moved. I was aware that something was horribly, terribly wrong. As I sat there, I felt more and more of the drug leaving my system, making me more aware of my situation.

These people were holding me against my will, without my permission. How could this be happening? I felt like I was the central character in a real-life horror film, not knowing my fate or what would happen next. I repeatedly tried to stand up and headed for the door, but each time I did, the guards would stand in front of the door, preventing me from exiting. I was weak and still partially drugged and definitely in no position to try to overpower them. I went back to the bed and fell asleep.

I next awoke in mid-stride, being walked through the now-open door down a hallway lined with various sized indoor Palm and Ficus Trees. I walked across a polished, marble, checkerboard, black and white floor; and then through an empty, upscale living room with several chairs and a sofa. This was a super-wealthy residence, filled with both classic and modern artwork hanging on the walls and several sculptures. They were made from wood and bronze, all primitive Giacometti-type tall, thin sculptures.

Even though I could never really see the Perpetrator's faces completely, I could tell they were young. Most of them seemed to be between the ages of twenty-one and thirty-five and they wore Carnival masks—although the guards and a few others wore full-faced masks. All of these masks were identical, with glowing red eyes that were most likely tiny, battery-powered light bulbs.

I knew that these were people and not aliens or monsters. I'm sure they were trying to convince me, under the influence of powerful, hallucinogenic drugs, lack of sleep, and the fear of being murdered or sacrificed, that they were actually demons.

I was escorted down a staircase into a dark, small room somewhere beneath the house. Here, they attempted mind conditioning, using bright white strobe lights and flashing red lights. It was similar in some respects to the conditioning done to the main character of the movie, *A Clockwork Orange.* My head was held in place by a simple restraint system which prevented me from turning, and forced me to look straight ahead at a screen. Terrible images were projected onto it; some images were drawings of monsters and demons. Others were live video clips of people being tortured and murdered. I was completely terrified and kept hoping to myself that this was really some nightmare from which I would wake up. Nothing could have been further from the truth.

The words and images flashed by on the screen and set off vast amounts of adrenalin in my body and created deep, long-lasting feelings of hopelessness and fear. Recorded screams and echoes were pumped into my head through acoustic headphones.

These sessions would last several hours. I was then returned to another room in a different part of the house to recover. This constant changing of locations under the influence of drugs like Scopolamine or Rohypnol is an attempt to further confuse the Victim to the point where nothing makes sense and no order exists. This conditioning process was then repeated over and over, draining me and leaving me on the edge of sanity and an emotional breakdown.

This elaborate process of abduction, drugging, and force-conditioning is called *creating a slave.*

Somewhere, deep down within my intuition, I had a feeling that if I could just make it through one more session, eventually all of this grueling torture would end.

I have no memory of any sexual abuse done to me, ever, at any time, although research indicates that Targeted Individuals are often sexually humiliated and abused during abductions. If anything did happen to me, I'm glad I don't remember it. However, something may have happened to me and was likely filmed or photographed; the footage could—in all likelihood—be floating around for sale on some torture website on the Internet. This is a common occurrence associated with this crime. Carefully arranged videos and staged photographic images taken of the Targeted Individual may surface long after the abduction, displaying him or her in compromising situations and circumstances. These images may contain children, animals, and illegal drugs—anything that could potentially destroy a Target's life and permanently tarnish their reputation.

At one point of my abduction, I was escorted into a large room in the mansion, where there were about fifty people attending a cocktail or dinner party. Everyone there, men and women alike, was wearing ordinary clothes, but all were wearing Carnival masks. These people were, again, *all Asian.* Waitresses in revealing outfits and wearing small carnival masks, only covering a portion of their faces, served food on silver trays.

I was left in the middle of the room, on the floor. The Scopolamine was intense and everything seemed to be swirling and melting. I was partially paralyzed. I felt like a lion or some animal that had been tranquilized: aware of my surroundings, but unable to walk or function as normal. People would walk by and just stare and laugh at me.

I recognized Brian there. He stood beside a Palm Tree and watched me through the palm leaves, partially obstructing my view of him. I wanted to ask him to help me, but I was unable to even speak at that point. A waitress passed by me at one point and offered me beautifully prepared sushi rolls, artfully displayed on palm leaves on a doily-covered silver tray. I just looked at her and shook my head *no*.

I could hear everyone talking at once. Conversations blended into each other and strange, alternative music was playing in the background. I was terrified beyond explanation.

I noticed my shirt was off. I just held it over the front of my body, unable to actually put it back on. *What was my shirt doing off? What was I doing here? Why was I being subjected to this barbaric torture and abuse?* Again, I was overwhelmed by the drug they had given me and as I sat on the floor, I began to perspire. Then, I became drenched in sweat. My head was pounding and I collapsed back onto the floor, unconscious.

Later, I would recall these and other memories, but only in fragments. I would only be left with small clues with many pieces of this elaborate puzzle missing.

༄ Chapter Four ༄

What is Happening To Me?

"Any sufficiently advanced technology is indistinguishable from magic."
Arthur C. Clarke. Profiles of the Future,
1961 (Clarke's Third Law)

The following is an excerpt from an article describing in detail how human beings are being implanted by the military, shadow governments, and the criminal underworld. This describes the procedure for implants for the ears only, although similar methods are used for implants that are installed elsewhere on the human body.

This article was reportedly written by an ex-C.I.A. agent and was posted anonymously on the Internet. The author's name and address were not mentioned. Further investigation of this article revealed that it was written by a doctor from the State of California familiar with this method of implantation.

THE PROCESS: How Implants Are Put Into the Victim's Body

The vast, interwoven, global network of criminals is without conscience. They are capable of mind control, murder, torture, and terrorism. A general description of these criminals and a recognized term for them is, "The Organization."

The chosen Victim is drugged through food, drink, or directly exposed to Ether gas within his or her own home. Illegal, covert surgery is either performed in the Victim's house or apartment or they are alternately moved to an undisclosed location. Surgery can also be performed in a van parked close to the Victim's residence. The Victim is caught completely off guard; and they are fully anesthetized while surgery or multiple operations are performed—all without the Victim's knowledge or consent.

A small cosmetic surgery cut or incision is made behind one or both of the Victim's ears. These small cuts are designed to heal quickly, without stitches by using a cosmetic surgery aid known as Dermabond. The incisions in the future, when healed, will resemble a natural fold in the skin. Then, a tiny plated electrode is slid beneath the skin, on top of the skull. Using EEG technology, this tiny repeater or transmitter can, at the speed of light and in real time, record and send out the signal coming from the human being's brain within the pre-speech center. The Victim who has these implants installed can now, with the aid of a converter capacity computer system, actually have their every thought read in real time and as they occur. A tiny speaker is inserted within each ear canal which enables the controller or Perpetrator to hear all sounds which the Victim hears, also in real time.

Using a complex system known as *silent subliminal sound technique* with a powerful low frequency speaker the unwitting Victim will now have thoughts placed into their brain. This is accomplished with the use of a hypnotist at a subconscious level. Now the Victim's thought can not only be read, but notions and thoughts can be relayed back into the Victim's brain.

It sounds like something out of a science fiction movie, but it is real. This technology has been around for a long time and it's constantly being upgraded, refined, and with greater capabilities and capacities. Some include neural implants which, with the use of a special gun-like device, are injected through the nasal cavity and inserted directly into the hypothalamus portion of the brain.

It's disgusting to fathom that a crime so widespread and so common has eluded detection for so long, so secretly. It is literally Hitler's Human Behavior Experimentation Program, taken several levels beyond.

The Aftermath of My First Abduction

I could not imagine anything worse than being held captive for a week by criminals. I did not know it then, but this process would happen to me at least six more times over the next nine months.

I awoke in my apartment, on what felt like the next

morning. I had the worst headache of my life and I felt like I had the mother of all hangovers. My apartment was a mess, with sheets and pillows everywhere. I still had my clothes on, although one shoe was on and the other was under a blanket across the bedroom.

What had happened? I thought and thought, and suddenly I remembered. It was like remembering things from a party where you had way too much to drink the night before. Some portions of my memory were blacked out.

I knew I had been drugged, and the effects of this drug were still very much present in my system. I looked over at my phone and saw a big, flashing message telling me that I had twenty-two messages. The clock read January 17. The last day I remember before my abduction was January 11. I had been gone for an entire week: a week of missing time, unaccounted for. I had missed doctor's appointments, a guided mountain climb with a friend, and a first date with a pretty young lady. My parents and sisters were very worried about me and had left several messages on my answering machine.

A package had arrived in my mailbox down in the lobby of my building. It contained a screenplay that was written by a Japanese writer, at least judging by the name, which I still cannot remember. Written on the front cover of the screenplay was the writer's name; then something else: It read "Directed by Sean Penn."

I remember my old neighborhood acquaintance, Brian, telling me that he knew a screenwriter that cooked for or knew

Sean Penn in some capacity, either for his family or catering at a restaurant that the actor had invested in. I only glimpsed at the script, I could tell this was not only a very amateur screenplay in terms of writing, but also in presentation. It had a fancy, serrated edging and the writing was not great. Only inexperienced screenwriters use fancy covers, artwork and illustrations, or catchy, colorful presentations. Real screenwriters—Hollywood's best— use a simple, solid color index stock (white, usually 110#), and nothing appears on the cover—not even the title. I also knew that somehow, this script was sent to me as some kind of message.

I telephoned Brian and asked him about my situation. I caught him completely off guard and he quickly became very reluctant to speak with me. I asked him this simple question, repeatedly: "Why would anyone want to drug and abduct me?"

He got very mad and replied, "Because when my friends asked you if you would like to cook with them in their kitchen or restaurant, you never called them back or even responded."

I was never asked if I wanted to cook in a restaurant. Brian was *gaslighting* me—trying to make me believe something that never happened.

After that, I tried to call him several more times that day, and as soon as he heard my voice, he would hang up. Before this, Brian had always been very nice to me—polite and seemingly a good acquaintance. Now he was acting very guilty. Finally, I got him on the phone and I began asking him questions.

He kept repeating, over and over, "Dude, I have not even

seen you since last September at my art show."

I knew I was the Victim of a crime of some form. I had to tell the police. I lived only a few blocks from the nearest police station.

I never went to the police because I did not yet have any proof that anything had happened to me, nor did I tell Brian that I saw him at my abduction, knowing he would only deny it.

I took a quick shower and got dressed. I noticed some very tiny cuts in the same places on both hands, but I didn't think much about it. I figured I had fallen or scratched them on something during my abduction.

If I had known the truth, I would have looked at these tiny cuts, closer. They were, in fact, not just cuts or common scratches, but tiny, precise, surgical incisions. However, at that point, my focus was in telling law enforcement of my predicament. It would not be until one year later that I would recognize the full extent of my fate and all that had happened to me.

I called a private investigation firm and explained what had happened to me. I spoke to them for about twenty minutes for a free consultation. They told me that it sounded like I was drugged with Scopolamine and that the Perpetrators, suspected Japanese or Asians, were most likely part of a very large global network gang known as the Yakuza.

The Yakuza is one of the most powerful gangs or organized crime groups—or mafias—in the world today. One of the private investigators told me that their team might be able to help me, but I would have to give them $10,000 as a retainer fee to even start the investigation. I told them I would think about it and thanked them for their advice and suggestions. They also recommended getting a blood test immediately.

I left my apartment building and started walking towards the police station. While walking, I thought about how I would explain my abduction and my being drugged to law enforcement. I knew the first thing they were going to ask me was, "Do you have any evidence or proof?"

I read that Scopolamine and Rohypnol and similar drugs, leave the system very quickly and can only be detected for up to twenty-four to forty-eight hours after exposure. Blood tests are the best way to confirm and verify covert drugging. Although, simply changing a single chemical component of a drug can make detection and identification even more difficult.

I changed direction and started to walk towards the hospital instead. Cedars-Sinai Hospital was only three blocks from my apartment. I went into the emergency room and asked for a blood test to confirm my suspicions. I had brought the screenplay that was anonymously sent to me in the mail as proof of a potential suspect. I entered the emergency room, signed in, and then took a seat. There were other people ahead of me, so I had to wait my turn.

Finally, three hours later at approximately 6:00 p.m., I was called into a small room where I attempted to explain my need for a blood test. The doctors were all very dismissive of the story I told them. They asked if I had a history of mental health problems or a drug habit. I told them I was a Victim of abduction and involuntary drugging.

I was left in a very difficult position. None of the doctors or nurses I spoke with believed me. They did not even check my body to see if I had been sexually abused and refused to give me the specific blood test I requested for Scopolamine or Rohypnol. They said that I must be kept at the hospital for observation.

They gave me some kind of medication to calm me down, and it sedated me. I had to wait many hours in the admittance department. They took everything away from me: my wallet, my cellphone, my shoes, and also my screenplay—my only evidence. They put everything into a plastic bag, and then placed it into a secured storage area.

I was sent to the psychological evaluation area, also known as "the psych ward." Here I had come into the hospital asking for a blood test, now I was put on an involuntary seventy-two hour hold, pending further evaluation. Talk about adding insult to injury. How could this be happening to me? I told the doctors the truth. I even knew what they drugged me with or what I suspected was used on me.

Now I was a patient, wrongly held against my will. Because they had taken away my money, spare change, credit cards, and my cell phone, I had no way of contacting my parents. My nightmare was about to get much worse and there was nothing I could do about it.

At this point it is hard to say what really happened to me at Cedars-Sinai Hospital.

The doctors in the emergency room knocked me out with a shot of some kind of general sedative. The next thing I remember is waking up at about 2:00 p.m. the next day, groggy and out of it.

Was it possible that the abduction was a set up to get me into the hospital where possible surgeries were done on me without my knowledge or consent? Was this a product of the shadow government, made to look as though a satanic cult had abducted me? Or was this whole crime really committed by criminals using secret, black-market-purchased government classified human experimentation information? How deep was this secret rooted?

The Targeted Individual (the Victim) is left with many unanswered questions and put in a position that leaves him or her defenseless and without credibility.

Here, I was being held with seriously mentally ill people: psychotic, depressed, delusional, paranoid, schizophrenic, and deranged individuals. "Mentally disturbed" would be an understatement in describing the kind of people who surrounded me.

Because I arrived at the emergency room with only the contents of my pockets, the screenplay as evidence, and the clothes on my back, I was now forced to wear a pair of hospital pants and cotton top that tied together in the back. I was now a patient; I was forced to take medication to calm and relax me and to help me "focus."

The Invisible Crime - Michael F. Bell

Every morning I would sit in a small side room off the main ward where a group of doctors and fellow student-doctors, would ask me questions and evaluate me. I did not like being asked to repeat my strange story over and over. The doctors would always ask the same thing: "Why would anyone want to abduct you?" I would always reply, "Why do people do any of the terrible things they do every day? Why does a man abduct, rape, and then kill a five-year-old girl? I don't know, but it's happening somewhere every day, with no end in sight. Why do people murder, torture, sexually abuse, and intentionally harm total strangers every day? I don't know the answers to these questions. You would have to ask the people that actually do these things; my answers are mere speculation. I can tell you one thing: anyone who does any of these evil things is sick, seriously disturbed, and is a menace to society. These types of people are sociopaths and psychopathic. That is the only answer I can give you, no matter how many times you ask me. You are doctors; you know the answer to these questions better than I do. I was drugged, abducted, most likely sexually abused, humiliated, and tortured. I do not know why someone or some people would do this; you would really have to ask them."

While I was held in the psych ward at Cedars-Sinai Hospital, my parents did not know where I was. After repeated calls to the police and hospitals, they located me. I had explained my story to my parents and they believed me. My parents and sisters found me after I was in the hospital for five days.

Up until then, I was made to participate in group meetings and art and music classes. I was served and ate terrible food.

Something was being done to the food; it was corrupted with some form of medication. After each meal, I would become unusually drowsy. Another patient informed me that they often medicate patients' food without their knowledge or consent.

Each day that passed by, I became more and more frustrated with being there. On the sixth day, my sister in San Diego, California called and threatened to sue the hospital if I was not released immediately.

Interestingly, I was released an hour later. My personal items were all returned to me, except for the screenplay. They had put my only evidence, the screenplay that was sent to me by the Japanese writer, in security storage. When I asked for it back, the security officer denied any knowledge of it and it was not included on my list of personal possessions.

Obviously, it was removed by someone connected to my crime. Corruption is evident in all aspects of society; even judges, police, doctors, and lawyers could be corrupt. People will do *anything* for money. Everyone has their price and anyone can be a whore for money. It has always been this way and it will continue, forever.

I walked back to my apartment and I felt glad to be out of the psych ward. The Four Seasons Hotel was only two blocks from my apartment, so I decided to have dinner there that night to celebrate being on the "outside" again.

When I returned to my apartment, I was reminded of all that had happened to me there. My family suggested that I move, preferably out of Los Angeles. My father has always said, "People in California are wacko; generally they have unrealistic lifestyles." I could not defend this. I knew he was right.

For those who have never been to California, there is only one nice thing about it—the weather. The weather was perfect, every day. When they shoot a movie or someone plans an outdoor wedding, they don't even bother with a backup plan in case it rains because it rarely does. Briefly in November, December, and January it may rain for a few days. The entire rest of the year is sunny, warm, and beautiful. If it wasn't for the weather, there would be no reason to live in Los Angeles. Gangs, drugs, illegal immigration, endless auto traffic and pollution, and an extremely high crime rate are all good reasons to stay away from Southern California. But, I still wanted to sell a screenplay to a major studio. I could not leave without trying just a little longer.

I started looking for another apartment in Los Angeles. Before I moved, I was still very frightened about the possibility of someone coming back to my apartment; so, every night I would barricade the front door with couches and furniture, so no one would be able to enter. Then, each morning, I would have to put all the furniture back where it belonged. It was a pain to do this every day, but it was better than the alternative—being victimized again.

I thought that my case was a one time, isolated incident, but I also thought it would be prudent to move and live somewhere else. I found a nice, but expensive apartment in Brentwood on Montana Avenue.

The Invisible Crime - Michael F. Bell

I lived across the street from the apartment Ron Goldman had lived in on the night he was murdered, and just five blocks from the house where Nicole Brown Simpson was murdered fourteen years earlier.

It was now a nice, quiet neighborhood, and all the stores including Starbucks, Peet's Coffee, and Whole Foods Market were only two blocks away. I could walk to the gym, the post office, and all the restaurants, so I would leave my car safe and sound in the underground parking lot beneath my building.

The first month was very enjoyable and I was able to get some good writing done. There were several very attractive young ladies who lived in my new apartment complex. I wanted to ask a couple of them out on a date, but I knew from past experiences that this was generally a recipe for disaster. Also, if I had put myself on the line and been turned down, seeing that same girl in the hall or lobby in the future would be tense and uncomfortable; so I decided to resist temptation.

There was a pool on the roof which had a great view of the area. I would sit poolside almost every day reading and listening to the radio and planning my next screenplay or thinking up ways of improving the one I was working on.

While sitting by the pool on the roof, I noticed something unusual occurring on a fairly regular basis. A black, unmarked helicopter would fly into the airspace directly above me. It would just hover, sometimes for as long as thirty minutes. There are so many news and police helicopters in Los Angeles; I really didn't pay much attention to this at first. After several weeks of this unusual and loud event, I called the local news stations and the local police to inquire. They all informed me that it was neither a news or police helicopter.

This is actually another harassment technique known as aerial or *air stalking*. This activity, when repeated over time, is bothersome and a nuisance. This had actually started happening to me back at my first apartment, but I always thought it was the news covering a local car accident or perhaps the police just patrolling the neighborhood. Imagine the time and cost involved to accomplish such harassment. That is another thing about being a Targeted Individual (Victim): Perpetrators will spare no expense to achieve their goals of instilling fear and paranoia in their Victims.

There are several popular techniques used by organized stalkers. *Brighting* is a very common method of letting a Target know that they under constant surveillance. Flashing the high beams of a car while either following the Target's vehicle or turning the bright lights on as the Target's vehicle drives in the opposite direction or lowering the high beams to the low position even in the middle of the day, is very distracting. At first, the Target will not even notice this form of harassment; however, over time and with repetition, it will inevitably frustrate the Target to the point where they will become angry.

Other harassment techniques include *crowding* the Target in public places, cutting in front of the Target in line and making him or her wait much longer than necessary. *Entrapment* is an extremely effective method of getting a Target arrested or even institutionalized. By baiting, luring, or taunting a Target into a confrontation, other surrounding Perpetrators will suddenly appear and give the police false information about the Target either by lying or planting incriminating evidence on his or her own person, residence, or vehicle. Such incriminating evidence may include illegal drugs, firearms, or elements of an explosive device, or even covertly drugging the Target to cause a staged automobile or on-the-job accident.

Street theater is a very common harassment technique. It can involve crowding the Victim while standing in line at a store or having kids play noisy games outside the Victim's residence. If the Victim were talking to a friend about a new movie that involved robots for example, later that day—maybe while in a store—a child wearing a shirt with "Robots" printed on it or a "Transformers" T-shirt might cross their path. Recently, I was talking to another Victim about the North and South Poles and the Hollow Earth Theory. Later that day while she was in the local library, a twelve-year-old boy came by, dragging his feet to get her attention; he was wearing a T-shirt that had the words "South Pole" printed on it.

When a Target passes by a group of Perpetrators, they may discuss things out loud that only the Target would know about or that are similar to a recent conversation that the Target had with another person, word-for-word. Small, but perceptible distractions such as: whistling, humming, sneezing, coughing, tapping of one foot, jingling of keys, an evil and intimidating stare, and accidentally bumping into the Target are all subtle things that are designed to annoy and intimidate the Target. Yes, sometimes these things will happen naturally or by coincidence. When these things happen all day, every day, it is a form of ongoing stalking and harassment. If coincidences continue to happen, the word coincidence loses all meaning. If everything is a coincidence, then there is no such thing as a coincidence.

I kept doing more and more research both at the Beverly Hills Library and on the Internet. I had read that Perpetrators will often rent adjacent apartments to the Target or completely surround them, above and below and in neighboring buildings. Imagine, again, the enormous expense it would take to maintain 24/7 surveillance on someone and never get caught, never leaving behind a shred of evidence. It's easy to see that if this happened to you that you would quickly realize there is nowhere to hide, no safe zone, or no escape from the prison your life had become.

I continued to feel ill and nauseous, with terrible headaches. Car stereos would be turned on and cranked up with loud, thumping music each night just as I was going to sleep. I also read about real devices available on the Internet, like through-the-wall radar systems that allow people to actually watch someone through an adjacent apartment wall or while looking down through a floor to spy on the Target living below them.

The most fearful sounding thing I had read was something called *directed energy*. Directed energy is an invisible form of energy: usually ultrasonic, electromagnetic, microwave, or another source.

The Invisible Crime - Michael F. Bell

This directed energy can cause the body to overheat very quickly and causes profuse sweating. It can cause pinpoint pain, like "bee stings" on specific spots anywhere on the human body. It can also be used on the pets of Victims. Directed energy can cause an enlarged heart from the low level, constant and continuous microwave energy. Physical burns, facial rashes, bruises, welts, and sore, tired, aching muscles are all side effects of directed energy. If focused on the eyes, the Target will experience sore eyes and blurry vision, or even permanent blindness.

Many other strange things were happening to me at my apartment in Brentwood. I would make a doctor or dentist appointment thinking it was for the next morning. When I arrived at the office, the nurse would say, "Where were you? You never showed up. Your appointment was on Monday morning; today is Friday." This continued to happen to me on at least six or seven separate occasions.

I was being drugged, most likely at night, and taken to some unknown, remote location; then I was returned to my apartment several days later. This covert drugging method can be accomplished using a variety of techniques. Here is a short list of the most common ways of surreptitious drugging:

1) Food or beverage drugging.

2) Direct drugging by injection or Ether or Chloroform exposure.

3) Drugs sprayed directly into the Target's bedroom at night while they are sleeping.

4) Remote/release. This is probably the most sophisticated form of covert drugging. When the Target is away from their residence, several Perpetrators will keep an eye out for the Target. Perpetrators are also experts at gaining access through unforced entry to the Target's residence. They usually have their own set of keys, but are also proficient at picking locks and bypassing security systems. A small canister, usually containing Ether gas is placed out of sight, often beneath the Target's bed. Later that night, when the Target is asleep, the small canister is activated remotely using wireless technology, filling the room with Ether gas. After a short period of time, the Perpetrators then can do whatever they like to the Target. For women, this usually involves rape or sexual abuse.

5) Blow darts are still used to this day to drug Victims and can contain any drug the Perpetrators choose—even lethal poisons.

I began feeling more and more frightened about my situation. The police would not help me, and both the CIA and the FBI refused to assist me with this crime of organized stalking that was being perpetrated on me.

My vision had changed completely, distorted with light sensitivity and even small hallucinations, as if the ground were moving or melting.

A simple walk to Starbucks or Peet's for a cup of coffee each morning became increasingly stressful. Passing drivers would honk their horns at me, flash their lights at me, yell obscenities out the window, or give me the finger as they drove past. People on the street would give me obvious dirty looks, while others would laugh long and hard at me as I passed them. Each time I left my apartment I would always put a tiny piece of paper tape at the very top of the door, knowing that if it was torn when I returned, my security had been breached. I would pile up furniture around the inside of the door, with glasses and plates perched in precarious positions so if somebody did try to enter, they would inevitably knock them all over, letting me know that someone had entered in my absence.

Every two or three weeks, as if on some kind of schedule, I would be drugged and there would be several days missing that I could not account for. After these episodes, I began to again notice tiny cuts on my arms, my face, and my legs and feet. They really looked like the kind of scratch one receives when brushing by a bush or a tree branch when out hiking. I did a lot of hiking and could only think this is how I received all of these cuts.

One afternoon, I brushed my teeth and immediately could feel some kind of drug enter my system. My vision became cloudy and the next thing I realized, I had been led out of my building and locked out. I was left walking around the front of my building wearing only my boxer shorts and a shirt.

Imagine the humiliation and embarrassment I experienced, even completely drugged out of my mind. The building manager called the police, who let me back into the building and back into my apartment. My keys were sitting on a desk right near the door. It was also at this time that my strong intuition told me that the manager of my building was somehow involved with my situation.

The Invisible Crime - Michael F. Bell

When a Target is drugged and receives involuntary implants, there is also time included for the cuts or incisions to heal. Today's high-tech, organized stalkers will hire retired surgeons or simply ones that like to take bribes and hush money.

Biomedical implant technology is now increasing its capabilities and advancements at an alarming rate—which doubles every five years. Today's implants continue to get smaller with greater capabilities and are now made from materials like conductive resins and polymers that are extremely difficult to detect and locate. Once again, there are two main types of biomedical implants, the first of which is surgically placed in a fixed position in the body. The second type of implant is one that is inserted or injected with a syringe. These implants are not in a fixed position and often migrate far away from the point of insertion. So, even if you are lucky enough to find the syringe injection mark, the implant will most likely have moved and rooted itself into a new area.

Neural implants that have been injected into a Target's brain via the nasal cavity are electronic transmission devices that can be uplinked. People on torture websites can actually pay money to spy on, monitor, and torture a perfect stranger.

It has been estimated that the United States Government spends ten times the amount of money on biomedical research and development than it does on its nuclear development programs. Since 2000, the United States Government has spent nearly a trillion dollars on research and development alone. That does not even include the price of the current wars being waged in the

Middle East.

Targets also may become Victims of *staged automobile accidents.* Even though I had moved to Brentwood, my membership at my local gym still had several months left on it before it expired, so I had to get up every other day very early to beat the morning crowd. I usually left my apartment at about 4:30 each morning.

One morning, as I was driving down a dark Wilshire Boulevard, a van pulled up alongside of me. Someone threw a cinder block wrapped in plastic at the passenger side of the car and my air bags immediately deployed. Glass and plastic debris swirled through the air, along with a cold rush of the outside air. I pulled over for a moment to the side of the road and a man silently walked up to my car and sprayed something in my face. It stung at first, and I quickly became disoriented. They had drugged me with something again. The same man picked up the cinder block lying next to the side of the road, threw it into the van, and quickly drove away.

I didn't know what to do. Were these people going to kill me? Were they trying to scare me to death? I have a strong suspicion that what they had sprayed me with was Scopolamine. I remember the way I felt when they abducted me, and this was the same drug—I recognized its effects. I was near a freeway entrance and so I got onto the freeway and just drove. I didn't know where I was going, but I felt I had to keep moving.

The Invisible Crime - Michael F. Bell

I pulled off the freeway approximately fifteen minutes later and then parked in front of a 7-Eleven convenience store. I just sat there not knowing what to do or who to tell; who would believe me? By chance a police car stopped at the store and noticed my deployed airbags and the damage to my Mercedes-Benz. Even though I was disoriented, I was able to carry on a conversation with the police officers who questioned me about the condition of my car. They searched the cars for any contraband and realized I was not drunk, but they took me to the nearby Del Amo Hospital in Torrance, California. There, I was sedated and put into another psychiatric ward. I explained to the doctors what had happened, but they said that maybe I was trying to hurt myself and that I should be kept for up to fifteen days for observation.

Here I was in another mental ward with severely disturbed individuals, for no reason. A criminal group had set me up to make it look as though I had tried to take my own life. A lingering side effect of Scopolamine is slurred speech. I called my parents and told them about this latest incident and they could not believe it. My mother left our family home in North Carolina where she runs an alpaca farm. She stayed for almost a week, visiting me every day. *What was happening to my life? How would this all end and when?*

Once again I was in a psychiatric ward, forced to take medication that I did not need, participate in group meetings, and held against my will in a place that was made for people who had really lost their minds.

I did what I was asked to do and tried to maintain a good

attitude, despite the extreme set of circumstances. I knew that the more I participated in the activities they had planned, the quicker I would get out.

After fifteen days, they decided to release me. I went back to my apartment, terrified of what would come next. Whatever this thing was that I was a Victim of, was surely not just going to stop and go away. My automobile insurance carrier at the time, Wawanesa, did a thorough investigation and after four months, they determined that I was indeed telling the truth. I was one-hundred percent *not* at fault. Their investigation confirmed what I had said all along: someone threw something at my car.

Two months later, I was parked near Starbucks in Brentwood and as I pulled out of my parking spot, a lady sped past a yield sign and clipped the front door of my car. She was clearly at fault; this time, the insurance company said that I was at fault. Now within just a few months, I was involved in two automobile accidents.

During the past year, I developed symptoms of a rarely heard of medical condition called Morgellons Disease. In short, skin parasites. I would get the feeling like something was biting my skin and that things were crawling in the hair on my head.

My parents thought it might be a good idea to go to UCLA Medical Center only a mile from my Brentwood apartment to have some medical tests performed. The day I was to check into the hospital, I was drugged again and arrived at the hospital in a very angry and irate state.

The Invisible Crime - Michael F. Bell

For the third time in five months, I was admitted to a psychiatric ward—this time at UCLA Medical Center. Here, I told them of my condition with skin parasites, a condition I thought I had contracted while on a mountain climbing expedition in a remote part of Mexico the year before. I was held for two weeks and finally released. Even though I had positive blood tests showing a trichinosis type of infection, the doctors thought it was all in my head. Little did they know how wrong they were. Later, I would be able to prove my condition.

The Invisible Crime - Michael F. Bell

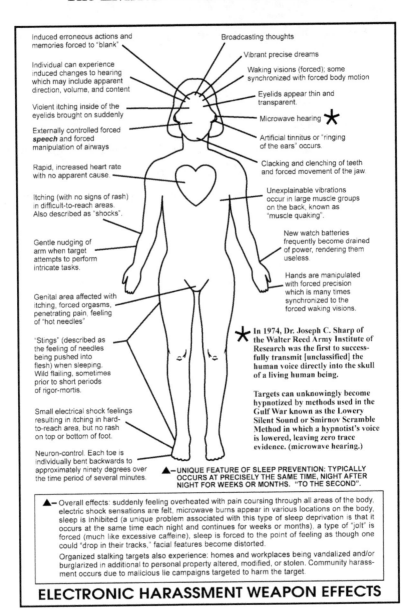

Induced erroneous actions and memories forced to "blank"

Broadcasting thoughts

Vibrant precise dreams

Individual can experience induced changes to hearing which may include apparent direction, volume, and content

Waking visions (forced); some synchronized with forced body motion

Eyelids appear thin and transparent.

Violent itching inside of the eyelids brought on suddenly

Microwave hearing

Externally controlled forced **speech** and forced manipulation of airways

Artificial tinnitus or "ringing of the ears" occurs.

Rapid, increased heart rate with no apparent cause.

Clacking and clenching of teeth and forced movement of the jaw.

Itching (with no signs of rash) in difficult-to-reach areas. Also described as "shocks".

Unexplainable vibrations occur in large muscle groups on the back, known as "muscle quaking".

Gentle nudging of arm when target attempts to perform intricate tasks.

New watch batteries frequently become drained of power, rendering them useless.

Hands are manipulated with forced precision which is many times synchronized to the forced waking visions.

Genital area affected with itching, forced orgasms, penetrating pain, feeling of "hot needles"

In 1974, Dr. Joseph C. Sharp of the Walter Reed Army Institute of Research was the first to success-fully transmit [unclassified] the human voice directly into the skull of a living human being.

"Stings" (described as the feeling of needles being pushed into flesh) when sleeping. Wild flailing, sometimes prior to short periods of rigor-mortis.

Targets can unknowingly become hypnotized by methods used in the Gulf War known as the Lowery Silent Sound or Smirnov Scramble Method in which a hypnotist's voice is lowered, leaving zero trace evidence. (microwave hearing.)

Small electrical shock feelings resulting in itching in hard-to-reach area, but no rash on top of bottom of foot.

Neuron-control. Each toe is individually bent backwards to approximately ninety degrees over the time period of several minutes.

▲—UNIQUE FEATURE OF SLEEP PREVENTION: TYPICALLY OCCURS AT PRECISELY THE SAME TIME, NIGHT AFTER NIGHT FOR WEEKS OR MONTHS. "TO THE SECOND".

▲— Overall effects: suddenly feeling overheated with pain coursing through all areas of the body, electric shock sensations are felt, microwave burns appear in various locations on the body, sleep is inhibited (a unique problem associated with this type of sleep deprivation is that it occurs at the same time each night and continues for weeks or months), a type of "jolt" is forced (much like excessive caffeine), sleep is forced to the point of feeling as though one could "drop in their tracks," facial features become distorted.

Organized stalking targets also experience: homes and workplaces being vandalized and/or burglarized in additional to personal property altered, modified, or stolen. Community harass-ment occurs due to malicious lie campaigns targeted to harm the target.

ELECTRONIC HARASSMENT WEAPON EFFECTS

66

The Invisible Crime - Michael F. Bell

Why Is This Happening to Me?

The big question that all Targets are asked is, *"Why?"*

Why would anyone go to such great lengths to harass someone? It is not logical and makes absolutely no sense; but, crime comes in many different forms—and it doesn't have to make sense. Sometimes, it's sadistic gratification or ritualistic torture. Crime happens, regardless of its reason. Crime doesn't have to be logical.

Why me? Why would someone spend so much energy and money and manpower focusing on making an innocent person's life a living hell? There is no simple answer to this question. Sometimes it's a matter of simply being at the wrong place at the wrong time or associating with people of a criminal background. Organized stalking by proxy and electronic harassment can be done for spite, jealousy, revenge, or even sport.

There is a general profile for Targets. They are usually single, live by themselves, are independent, and tend to be somewhat reclusive. A general age range for most Targets is between the ages of twenty-five and fifty-five years of age. These are not hard and fast rules, but it's a fairly accurate assessment.

I could not understand why I was being targeted. I had done nothing illegal or morally wrong. I had not slept with another man's wife or stolen or embezzled money. I was, by all accounts, a good and law abiding, innocent citizen.

The more I read about organized stalking, the more I became aware of the fact that this was exactly what was happening to me. After my week in Cedars-Sinai psychiatric ward, I began to also think there might be something wrong with me.

I went to my regular doctor and explained my situation to him as rationally as I could. He thought that it sounded like I had suffered a stroke and ordered an MRI of my brain, with and without contrast. The results were negative, but I kept the MRI CD and held on to it for future reference. Later, it would be this MRI CD which would end up helping me more than I could have ever imagined.

❦ Chapter Five ❧

Perpetrators: Who Are They and Who Funds Them?

"And there will be such intense darkness that one can feel it."
Exodus 10:21

Statistics show that at least seventy-five percent of all Targets do not know their Perpetrators. That means that most organized stalking is done by complete strangers, to complete strangers.

It is estimated that a large percentage of Perpetrators are unemployed—at least fifty percent. This explains why Perpetrators are always available, at any time. Harassing strangers is their job. The Perpetrators or Attackers are often paid in small amounts of money and have gas and other related expenses paid for by the group, gang, or criminal organization they represent. Some are paid in drugs or are trying to achieve a higher position within the organization.

69

Most Perpetrators are bottom-of-the-barrel low-lifes and substance abusers, often former criminals themselves, basically unfit for any regular job. Many Perpetrators were once themselves Targets, coerced to become Perpetrators to avoid further harassment.

What motivates a perfect stranger to harass another person completely unknown to them? Perpetrators are almost always given misinformation about the Targets they harass, such as: the Target is a pedophile or homosexual or that they pose a threat to the safety of the country. Sometimes the Perpetrators are told they are really spies whose plans include sabotaging the U.S. Government. If they're working for the shadow government or black operative groups, they may be paid well for their harassing and taunting of the Targets to which they are assigned. Some Perpetrators just participate for fun or kicks. These are deeply disturbed, psychotic, sociopathic, delusional, and depressed individuals.

There are basically two types of Perpetrators: *Operators* or *Controllers* are at the top of the group and usually select the Target. Additionally, they are in charge of giving orders to be carried out by the second group of Perpetrators—the *Grunts* or *Henchmen*. These are the ones who flash their high beam lights at Targets, honk their horns, or yell obscenities at the passing Targets.

In order to motivate the Henchmen, the Operators provide them with misinformation about the Targets. Often, pictures of the Target, taken while they were drugged during their abduction process, will show the Target in humiliating situations, sometimes involving small children or engaging in lewd sexual acts. Most of the time the low-end Perpetrator is given negative information about the Target that will further incite him or her, fueling the drive to torment the Target with greater intensity.

There is a third group of Perpetrators known as the *Sandmen*. These criminals usually operate in groups of three and are responsible for drugging the Targets, abducting them from their residences, and transporting them to an undisclosed surgery center. Often times, these Sandmen teams will perform the surgeries right in the Target's own residence, leaving nothing behind and no evidence, whatsoever. Sandmen teams may also perform surgeries in an unmarked van just outside the Target's residence.

How do I know all this is true? I have been studying and researching this subject for over seven years and I've read secret, hacked government reports. They all basically said the same thing: this is a secret criminal group, which operates above the law. Since they have access to all the latest, most expensive—and best—technology, their chances of getting caught continue to diminish.

Perpetrators are also famous for poisoning or murdering and mutilating a Target's pets or sexually assaulting and or murdering a Target's children or family members. Nothing could be more evil and diabolical than these groups of the Devil's workers.

If what has already been disclosed is not disturbing enough, pets of Targeted Individuals are often implanted with optic nerve implants and auditory implants.

Now, your beloved and cherished dog or cat, through the implant system, becomes an unwitting spy. Seeing and hearing all that the pet comes in contact with allows the Perpetrators to get an even closer look into the Targeted Individual's life.

Perpetrators are very cunning and sly. They will wait for the perfect moment to abduct or drug the Victim or to gain access to the Victim's home. In this respect, they can be compared to the hungry coyote that will wait outside a rabbit's den for days. When the mother rabbit finally leaves for food and water, the coyote invades the den and carries off and eats her young.

Prostitution, drug dealing, money laundering, illegal gambling, and racketeering provide huge incomes to the criminal organization.

A question that is often asked is: *Why is there no news coverage of this crime?* There is literally a media blackout on organized stalking, electronic harassment, and mind control.

Everything a Perpetrator wants to use on a Target is available on the Internet. Handbooks are available on the Internet with information on how organized stalking works, how electronic harassment is accomplished, and how government-developed mind control works.

Just go online and search for "buy electronic harassment devices." You may be amazed at all the websites and distributors that will appear.

The Invisible Crime - Michael F. Bell

Books on how mind control works and what drugs are most effective in accomplishing the most disgusting crimes are all available for purchase.

·

⟋ Chapter Six ⟍

Private Investigators

"If you can imagine something, chances are it already exists."

Michael Fitzhugh Bell

At one point or another, every Targeted Individual either hires a private investigator or asks one for advice on how to legally handle his or her situation and prove he or she is being harassed.

Just like everything else in life, there are good private investigators and bad ones. They are all willing to take your money, but none will promise you anything.

On October 6th, 2008, I was awakened from a sound sleep by a strange buzzing in my ears, similar to the sound old fashioned fluorescent light bulbs make. I also noticed that my teeth were vibrating. I ran to the bathroom and looked in the mirror and found about a dozen tiny red blisters on my lips and small red marks near both of my eyes. I was being hit with a strong beam of directed energy, most likely, electromagnetic or microwave energy.

Some Perpetrators will dismantle a microwave oven and remove the door, and from an adjacent apartment or residence, aim that oven at the Target's bedroom. The effects can be felt immediately: headaches, nausea, and blisters on the lips and around the eyes. Generally, the skin which is the most delicate shows signs of the microwave energy burns the soonest.

Another tactic is to install a directed energy device inside the Target's bedroom when he or she is away from home. Then, the device can be operated remotely from several miles to several thousand miles away, using a satellite system. Today, most directed energy devices are operated remotely using the cellular satellite system. That means a Perpetrator can monitor and torture a Target using a cell phone.

Covert cameras and listening devices are often installed in the Target's residence in his or her absence—often behind mirrors, within heating or air conditioning ducts, or even in the keyholes of doors throughout the residence. Go online to any spy shop website; you'll find it's possible to get countermeasure products that reveal hidden cameras, bugs, or hidden microphones. These devices are inexpensive and easy to use. You simply look through the viewfinder, which resembles a camera lens; any hidden camera or hidden transmitter will light up, even if the covert device is turned off at the time of inspection.

These covert cameras and bug finders are also extremely useful while staying at hotels or motels and cruise ships. It is very common for Perpetrators to install hidden cameras in hotel bathrooms and bedrooms. There are many websites which offer the viewer a peek into someone else's life for a hefty monthly fee.

Because the covert devices use wireless technology, it is difficult to prove where the source is located. If a Target does locate any hidden transmitters, cameras, or bugs, it is best to call local law enforcement right away and report the incident. Directed energy devices, which can be bought by anyone on the Internet, can also be installed somewhere on the Target's property— sometimes on the roof. When using a bug or camera detector, it is recommended to sweep the entire residence, inside and out. The same websites which sell electronic harassment and electronic torture devices also sell countermeasure devices to people who are being targeted. This is called working both sides of the street.

People will do anything for money. It's not uncommon to watch the local news and see that a store owner was shot and killed for fifteen dollars. There are many good and positive things in this world, but none of us should ever leave our homes without being aware of the danger and crime that lurks in the shadows all around us, every day.

I stopped driving my car unless absolutely necessary to avoid any more staged accidents. Luckily, my apartment in Brentwood was within walking distance to everything that I needed.

One morning I walked up the hill to the post office to mail a few letters. A convoy of Perpetrators followed me, honking their

The Invisible Crime - Michael F. Bell

horns and flashing their bright lights, revving their car engines and dropping them into a lower gear to make their cars as loud as possible. This is called *mobbing*, overwhelming the Target in an attempt to frighten and anger him or her.

On the walk back to my apartment, a short man of Hispanic descent was wearing a breathing mask as he blew leaves off of a driveway. He wore a backpack-style leaf blower. As I passed by, he looked me straight in the eye and aimed the leaf blower at my face; I could see that he was squeezing a small trigger near the handle of the machine.

I immediately jumped out of the way, but a small portion of the chemical he sprayed at me had gotten into one of my eyes. It stung; the vision in my left eye was slightly blurry for almost three days. The side of my face was also numb for the same amount of time. I wanted to confront the man and punch him for spraying me with this unknown drug or chemical; that is just what the Perpetrators would have wanted me to do. Then, I would have been arrested and ended up with a criminal record. And perhaps I would have been sued and lost my case to the very man who had intentionally sprayed me. So, once again, my hands were tied. There was really nothing I could do.

One night in October of 2008, I felt directed energy heating up my body, drenching me in perspiration; and then I felt the intense pain of the blisters now covering both the upper and lower lips and my eyelids. I fled my apartment the next morning, taking a flight from Los Angeles to my parents' house in Tryon, North Carolina. I was absolutely terrified; I was afraid for both my life and my health. It was also at this time that I noticed several small patches of white hair— not gray—on several places on the top of my head.

My parents were very understanding and let me stay with them. I had visited several times over the previous six months, trying to get away from my Attackers. Each time I returned to my apartment in Brentwood, the same patterns of strange events would repeat themselves: I was drugged, abducted, most likely sexually abused, stalked, and tortured.

I did a lot of research on the subjects of organized stalking and electronic harassment and I found a private detective in Idaho who is well known in this field. He had over thirty years of experience as an electronics expert and had worked with everyone from mafia organizations to Howard Hughes. His name was George Seymour, circa 60, and he knew more about this subject than anyone else in the world.

My father flew back to Los Angeles with me to clean out my apartment and helped me move my belongings into a large moving truck, which carried my car inside of it, as well. All of my possessions were then moved to a storage facility in North Carolina, not far from my parents' house.

My father flew back home to North Carolina and I flew to Salt Lake City, Utah. From there, I rented a car and drove to Pocatello, Idaho, to see the private investigator, George Seymour.

The first thing George said was that he needed all the money—up front, and in cash. The scanning for implants, interviews, and shielding technology he had for me would cost $4,000. He also said right from the beginning that he could make no promises and that he probably would not be able to stop the harassment I was receiving; he could offer me some good advice and provide me with some shielding countermeasures to help protect me from the directed energy from which I was being bombarded.

Every night, just as I was drifting off to sleep, I would receive a short, sharp electric shock. As I closed my eyes to go back to sleep, I would see swirling colors and Strobe light-type lights even with my eyes closed. Some Targets receive something called *V2K* or *Voice-to-Skull Technology*. With this technology, voices can be beamed directly into the Target's head, usually 24/7, causing severe sleep deprivation, depression, irritability, and complete lack of R.E.M. sleep which is essential for proper health, well-being, and a healthy immune system.

I was receiving what is known as *silent subliminal sound presentation.* I did not hear any voices, but I could hear a constant, continuous buzzing or humming sound with loud and disturbing tone bursts, interrupting my sleep.

I also noticed that I began experiencing strange, vivid dreams that were not natural. Certainly we all experience a weird dream from time to time, but these dreams were different. Usually they were often sexual or violent in nature. Within these dreams, it was always the same theme: I lost something, sometimes a girlfriend or misplaced keys. Frightening strangers would follow me and haunt me in these dreams. This is another technique the

Perpetrators use called *dream insertion* or the *dream machine.*

It's accomplished during the abduction process, either through EEG brain wave technology or implants which are inserted through the nasal cavity directly into the brain.

A device known as a pneumatic brain radio transsphenoidal injection-implantation tube, injects a neural spike radio transmitter into the hippocampus nerve part of the brain. This endoscopic pituitary surgery or injection into the soft tissue of the hypothalamus makes the Target a slave or robot.

While the Target is sleeping, a hypnotist hypnotizes the Target. Then, the Target's innermost secrets can be revealed. Perpetrators may ask questions using this subliminal, silent-sound presentation, completely invading the Target's privacy and personal life. Every thought can be read in real time using the cellular system. At the same time, they can insert or create false memories. Some memories can be deleted or erased completely without the Target even being aware this is occurring.

While staying at a Holiday Inn in Pocatello, Idaho, George and his girlfriend Dianne came over to my room and unloaded a lot of high-tech devices such as spectrum analyzers, frequency counters, and energy measurement equipment. George took about an hour and a half to completely sweep my body for possible implants. He said I didn't have any. George told me that when he does find an implant in a client, he said he feels like a doctor telling his patient that they have cancer. A company in Germany had custom made a blanket for him which was composed from silver and nickel. He gave the blanket to me—and the first night I used it, I felt immediate relief. This particular blanket-type of shield is an example of "passive shielding."

Next, he constructed what he referred to as an "electro-static egg." This was basically PVC tubing that surrounded my bed like a box. On each side, he hung a metallic emergency blanket which he hooked up to a small electrical transformer; if touched, you would get a small shock. This is an example of "active shielding." The first night using the electro-static egg, I slept great.

I spent five days with George and Dianne; they even invited me back to their house one night. George has seen thousands of clients over the years and I was only the second Target invited into his home.

George said right from the start that the best he could offer me was some relief from the *electronic harassment*—a phrase he is responsible for coining. He said that most likely my Perpetrators would eventually turn up the level of harassment and that the tools he sold to me—the blanket and the electro-static egg—would then only provide minimum protection.

A friend of mine once told me that she knew a private investigator and the first thing he told her was, "Don't trust anyone...including me."

ᥰ Chapter Seven ᥰ

Contacting Other Targeted Individuals

"You can remember a single deluge only but there were many previous ones."
Plato

One thing George Seymour did for me was put me in touch with a lady who lived in New York City; her name was Marcy Taylor. She was sixty-seven years old and had been experiencing V2K and electronic harassment for the past seven years. She was the Victim of some other tenants in her building who were mad at her because her apartment was rent controlled and she paid about twenty percent of what new, more recent tenants were paying for their monthly rent.

I told her that my vision was still damaged from the repeated druggings and would take over six months to return to normal. She, too, had been drugged and abducted and felt as though she had been implanted. She had also gone to George Seymour for a body-sweep; he told her that she didn't have any implants, either.

It cannot be said enough how quickly the implant technology is developing, constantly getting smaller, more efficient, harder to detect and locate, with ever-expanding capabilities.

Marcy made me feel better in many ways. It was nice to be able to speak with someone who not only understood what I was talking about, but who was a Victim as well. She said that over the years she had heard many different stories, but none more unusual than mine. Marcy said that mine was by far the weirdest story she'd ever heard.

Marcy put me in contact with another Victim—Sagitar, thirty-three years old, who lived in Madrid, Spain. I began emailing Sagitar on a regular basis, trying to figure out how we would get out from this terrible situation. Sagitar had studied electronics and had a background in science; he had also spent a year and a half in medical school.

In January, 2009, I travelled to Patagonia, Argentina, with my parents for a fishing trip. I was harassed and followed—even in South America. A man on the plane kept turning around and staring at me, and while waiting in the lounge before takeoff, he walked right up to me and faked sneezing twice—then gave me an ugly, dirty look. My parents, who sat right next to me, were completely unaware. While visiting a National Park in Patagonia, a woman pushed me down from behind and walked right past me without saying a word. Sometimes things happen by coincidence;

when these things continue to happen and you can start to anticipate them, this is no longer a mere coincidence. If everything is a coincidence, then coincidences do not exist.

Sagitar and I began using Skype and having long video conference calls, plotting how to escape from our tortured lives. After much independent research—both in libraries and on the Internet—I came to the conclusion that we had to have been implanted.

I spoke to a very famous Victim: Josh Messa, from New York. He had a website that was more extensive than any Internet site I'd seen. He sold countermeasure protection from directed energy on his website: special clothing, caps, and jammers. For $60, he had a small pendant-sized jammer that was to be worn around the neck. It would knock down most of the directed energy, but not all of it. A tiny motor inside the jammer case would spin at a very high rate of speed, which caused interference in the directed energy being beamed at the Target.

He had pictures on his website which showed scars behind the ears of several Victims. These scars were the result of implants which were installed deep in the ear canals. It was done using cosmetic surgery techniques; the resulting scars were difficult to see and were designed to look like natural folds in the skin.

After I ordered my jammer, I called Josh Messa one afternoon and briefly explained my situation to him. I told him that I had been swept for implants and that I thought I was receiving EEG technology, or brain wave electronic harassment. He told me that he did not believe in that technology, and most likely I had been implanted. He asked me to have my family or friends look behind my ears for scars. He said most likely I would find scars, exactly like the ones that he had posted on his website.

The next day, I asked my father to look behind each of my ears to see if I had any scars there. He answered very quickly, "Yes, you have scars behind both ears; they are identical and in the same location on each side."

I shaved my entire body, excluding my head, and went outside on a bright, sunny morning. I found a scar in my navel. Then, I found a scar between my right thumb and forefinger and another scar on the left hand in the same place. The more I looked the more scars I continued to find. I noticed there was a definite pattern to the scars. They were all symmetrical and corresponding to the same exact location on the opposite side of my body. I also observed that one scar on one side was always more pronounced and easier to find and locate than the one on the opposite side of my body.

There were scars everywhere and everyplace in between— even in my privates and between my fingers and toes, and on the insides and outsides of my wrists. My arms and legs and my hands and feet were covered with these tiny, white surgical scars. I had somewhere between one hundred and fifty to two hundred tiny white surgical scars from head to toe.

After this discovery, I immediately Skyped Sagitar in Madrid, Spain and told him of my findings. I told him where to look, and he discovered that he, too, had scars—all exactly in the same places that I did. He went to a radiologist in his town and the implant in his navel clearly showed up in an ultrasound image.

I asked a doctor in Spartanburg, South Carolina for an ultrasound, but he ordered the wrong area to be checked and my test turned out to be negative. I told Sagitar the problems I was having getting ultrasound tests done here in the United States and he invited me to Madrid to see his radiologist.

In Europe, it is much easier to get medical testing done. As long as you have the money, you can get just about any test done that you desire.

Three weeks later I was on a plane to Madrid, Spain. Sagitar met me at the airport. We rented a car and drove straight to the radiologist. He instructed me to take my shirt off and lie down on the table. He coated the ultrasound wand with some gel and pressed it to my navel. Within five seconds, he said in English, "There it is."

Before my trip, I had trimmed my eyebrows because I was beginning to look like Walter Cronkite or Andy Rooney. By mistake, I set the trimmer too close and I took off the entire eyebrow. Then, I noticed something strange—a scar had been hiding within my eyebrow. Now I had to shave off the other eyebrow to make them look even. Another scar had been hiding within my other eyebrow.

I asked the radiologist to please check both eyebrows for possible foreign bodies. He found foreign bodies in each eyebrow, identical to the one he found in my navel. All three were exactly one centimeter in length. The radiologist acknowledged these foreign objects in his report. Although he did not include it in his report, he noticed that all three foreign objects were sending out a frequency "as if they were alive."

Two days later I returned to the same radiologist and repeated the same ultrasound images. The foreign objects were still there in the same positions.

I returned to the United States the next day with my ultrasound images and the report acknowledging them in hand. I showed them to my regular family doctor, who ordered MRI images of the soft tissue on the back of the neck, the abdomen, and the brain orbits.

The radiologists at the MRI imaging center said my report was normal, but foreign objects could be seen everywhere. Now, I'm not a radiologist, but even a child could see the strange, dense, bright white objects hiding beneath each location where I had a scar. However, even if you have a screwdriver in your head and the word *Phillips* can clearly be seen, if the radiologist does not acknowledge it in his report, it is not officially documented and recognized.

Doctor after doctor refused to help me with the removal of any of my foreign bodies. There were my scars, the stories of my repeated abductions, and burn marks on my skin that had formed from the inside out—but still no one would help excise anything.

If a Target is lucky enough to find a surgeon to examine a

suspected foreign body that shows up on ultrasound or MRI images, it is extremely important for the Target to express how much pain and discomfort and sleep deprivation this foreign body is causing them. Otherwise, doctors will often leave a foreign body inside a person if it is not causing them sufficient pain, infection, or swelling.

The Target with strong ultrasound or MRI images suggesting a foreign body may also have to hire an attorney to assist them in getting the foreign body removed. If the Target gets lucky and finds a surgeon willing to remove the foreign object, they must remember to photograph it and have the doctor acknowledge what this foreign body is. If the doctor doesn't acknowledge an implant as a non-therapeutic device that was placed in the Victim without their knowledge or consent, then the entire process will be a wash and nothing will come from it. And, sadly, it cannot be used as evidence in a court of law.

I contacted a doctor in London, England, who had removed a microchip implant that was placed in her arm voluntarily, but then she wanted it removed. Evidently, there was a journalist vacationing in Baja, Mexico. She went to a nightclub that offered a credit-card-identifying microchip to be inserted in her arm. When she paid for anything at the resort, all she had to do was swipe her arm over a scanner and her drink or food or shopping would be paid for, eliminating the danger and concern of carrying money around in Mexico. After her trip, the idea of having a tiny electronic transmission device inside her body made her feel uncomfortable, so she had it removed by a well-known Swedish doctor in London, England.

Removing a microchip implant is not like removing a splinter or a shard of glass or a tiny piece of metal or plastic. Once an implant is installed, it takes anywhere from three to six months for the body to latch on to it. Tiny skin cells, nerves, and scar tissue form around the implant making it a part of your body. Because of this nest of surrounding skin tissues, removing the implant is not only difficult, but it is extremely painful and also expensive to have excised or cut out.

Doctors have the right to refuse service to anyone just like a restaurant or bar. No matter how much evidence you have or how great your pain, if you can't find a surgeon to remove a foreign object, you're stuck with it.

This surgeon originally agreed to remove my foreign objects, but then suddenly changed her mind. Again, it is most likely that someone from the shadow government or a criminal organization threatened her and told her not to help me.

Even if you can feel the implant beneath your skin with your fingers and can grab it, if you try to remove it yourself, they will lock you up in a psychiatric institution. That is the reality of this situation. I would estimate most people— around ninety percent that have been implanted—don't even know it.

This puts the Target into an impossible situation. This also is another thing that makes this the perfect crime. Even if the Target realizes they have been implanted, doctors are unfamiliar with this rapidly advancing micro-technology and refuse to believe the patient.

Marcy, the Targeted Individual from New York, told me of another Victim who lived about thirty minutes away from me in Spartanburg, South Carolina. We talked on the phone several times and Skyped each other occasionally. His name is David and he is fifty-five years old. He works as an engineer at the BMW plant near Spartanburg. He had also had seen George Seymour a year earlier than I had.

David had been suffering with this condition for about five years. We met for lunch one day and discussed all of our similarities and traded information. He has the V2K or voice-to-skull technology and also got attacked with a lot of directed energy. He says he knows who his criminals are, even where they live.

David made an interesting discovery: by using a Sony Digital Voice Recorder, he has been able to capture what his Perpetrators are beaming into his head.

Normally, only the Target can hear what the Perpetrators are saying, but with the digital voice recorder, David now had evidence that he is indeed a Victim of a highly evolved, secret technology—just as I am.

I bought a digital voice recorder and made several recordings in which I could hear people whispering and music playing in the background. However, even with this evidence, it is extremely hard to prove and expensive to hire a voice analyzer and an attorney to represent you.

The Invisible Crime - Michael F. Bell

Meanwhile, Sagitar had gone back to the radiologist and found another foreign object between his thumb and forefinger of his right hand. The radiologist realized that Sagitar and I were obviously Victims of a powerful and evil crime organization.

Sagitar has since been asked by that radiologist to not come back anymore concerning the foreign bodies. The radiologist was scared for his own safety, and did not want to risk the safety of his own life or that of his family.

Nobody likes to hear people complain, but I feel I must share with the reader what it is like to be a Victim of this technology. There is the gradual, almost imperceptible decline in health: premature skin aging, heart pains, sore eyes, and sore teeth—like when the dentist hits the nerve when he's drilling for a cavity. Aside from all of the many pains, stress, and anxiety that electronic harassment causes, there is the loss of your personal life. This condition will destroy your life at every level. Your family, your wife or husband, boyfriend or girlfriend won't understand what you are going through and eventually the relationship will end.

The very idea of someone monitoring your every move, every minute of every day, is also disturbing. Imagine every time you use the toilet, take a shower, share intimate relations with your wife, husband, or partner, someone else is watching right there with you, listening to every word you say—every thought you have. All you know and see is now being observed by a stranger, someone you don't even know. No matter how strong you are mentally, this kind of constant, continuous pestering and harassing will get to anyone…eventually. Sometimes for brief moments you become distracted, temporarily, but then come back to reality: *I'm a Victim*. Compounded with the electronic stalking accomplished with the cellular satellite system, a Victim's life can become unbearable.

Just two weeks after moving back to live with my parents at their house in North Carolina, the organized stalking and electronic harassment was elevated to a new level of torture.

I was getting larger and more intense microwave and directed energy burns all over my body. Microwave or directed energy burns are much different than an ordinary burn from an external heat source like a match or a lighter. These directed energy burns come from the inside out. That is to say the burn occurs within the lining of the skin. An ordinary external heat-source burn will blister immediately. A directed energy burn starts out looking like a scratch, then blisters about a week later.

This is something that cannot be faked by the Target doing it to himself. Some doctors may claim that I am making up this entire ordeal in order to gain attention. I think everyone seeks attention to some degree, but this was not the kind of attention or recognition that anyone would want or be proud of,

I am a writer and I believe that I have a very good imagination, *but not **that** good*. It is simply not possible to say that I invented all of this myself. There are too many other Victims who have no contact with each other, yet they share identical stories.

The Invisible Crime - Michael F. Bell

In Los Angeles, I was followed by only black or white cars that all had their high-beam headlights on, night or day. Here in rural, backcountry North Carolina, I was being followed and harassed by all kinds of vehicles, mostly beat-up pickup trucks. The Perpetrators here were what many would call Hillbillies or Rednecks. "Back in the day," these people would distill whiskey in the mountains, called *moonshine*. Today these people might be running Methamphetamine labs deep in the back-wooded areas of the mountains and thick overgrown forests. This is what happens in small towns all over the United States; it is a generalization, but it is happening and these are the types of individuals who perpetrate this crime. They are basically uneducated, not hirable, and undesirable; this is a surprisingly accurate observation.

One afternoon, I went to a local supermarket and I parked my freshly washed Mercedes-Benz just across from the entrance to the store. As I entered the store, two hillbilly youths exited and I watched them as they walked past my car. They intentionally brushed into it and looked back at me and laughed, taunting me.

I pulled my digital camera out of my pocket, and as they drove past me in their broken down pickup truck, I snapped a picture of their car and the license plate. As soon as the flash went off, the truck stopped and went into reverse very quickly. I went inside the store and stood next to the manager, knowing a confrontation was inevitable. These two thugs came inside the store, approached me, and then demanded the photo. I said that was never going to happen. I responded with, "Do you have a warrant?" They did not answer. I said, "Call the police." One of the thugs pulled out a cellphone and started dialing, but what he did not know was that I also had a cellphone blocker in my other pocket. His call never went through. They stormed out of the store and warned me, "You better watch it, Dude. You don't know who you are dealing with." I knew who I was dealing with: a couple of scumbag punks who would never be anything. I kept my mouth shut.

These were seriously deprived people who grew up poor and angry at the world. Now, I was the focus of their sociopathic anger and frustration. Although there were always new Perpetrators, they all came from the same can of bad worms. They were country boys and I was the kid from the city, now in their neck of the woods—on their turf. This is where the digital video camera really helped me. I carried it stealthily, non-intrusively, but it was my best weapon. The Perpetrators are all the same everywhere you go on this planet; they are all cowards, running away like little children as soon as trouble comes their way. My camera threatened them, and at the same time, helped me to regain a small piece of my life.

Hope becomes the Target's friend: hope that someday soon, somehow, all of this will be over. Hope that this heinous crime is finally exposed to the general public. Hope that one day life will be good again, filled with love and making fond memories and being able to laugh and smile and be positive, again.

Patient Mr.: Michael F. Bell.

To MD.:

ULTRASOUND

Echogenic Image linear of 10 milimetres slightly to the right of the navel, repeated in different days, It doesn't suggest to be metalic. (no reverberation).

In Orbit, left orbit, in the peripherics of the globe from the previous chamber and with it's most adyacent part to the later chamber image similar (in size) to the jost refered object.

Evaluate MRI orbit or skull to evaluate the area retroavriculor, mastoidevnn.

It hasn't been evidenced in torax, Quadricps, or intercostal spaces.

Paciente Don.: Michael J Bell

A/A Dr.

ECOGRAFIA

.   Imagen ecogénica lineal de 10 mm ligeramente a la derecha de ombligo, repetida en dias diferentes, no sugiere ser metálica (no reverberación).

En órbita izquierda en la periferia del globo desde cámara anterior y con su mayor parte adyacente a la cámara posterior imagen similar (en tamaño) a la dscrita. Valorar RM orbita o craneal para valorar área retroauricular, mastoidea.

No se ha evidenciado en tórax, cuádriceps, o espacios interdigitales.

Above is documentation from a well-known radiologist in Madrid, Spain. I have included both the original written in Spanish and a handwritten translation in English. This official documentation acknowledges three foreign bodies, one within each eyebrow and a third in my navel.

96

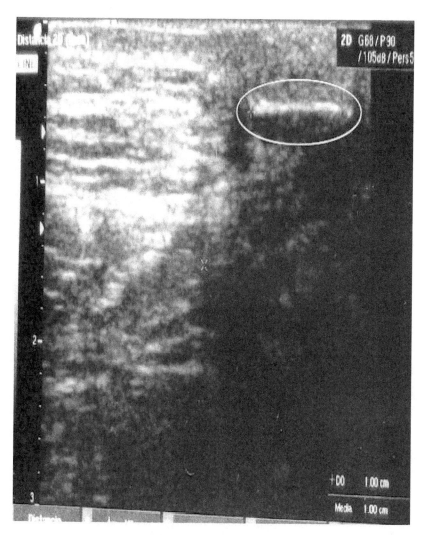

A linear foreign body in my navel can be seen here in an ultrasound image.

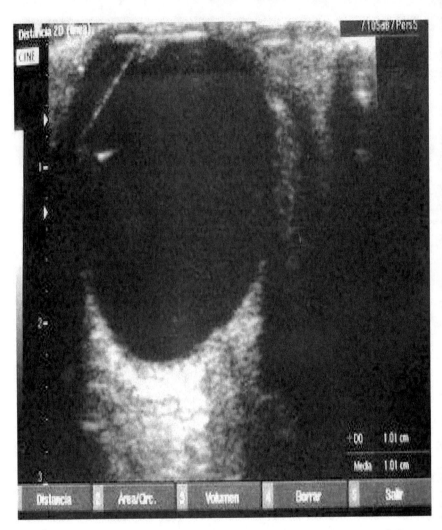

A linear shaped foreign body can be seen at the top of the ultrasound image, just above my right eye.

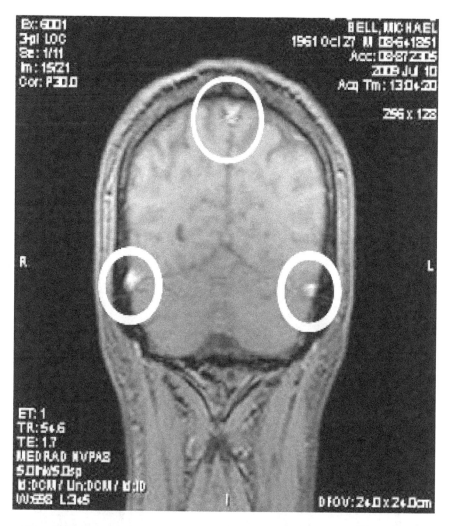

Three bright white foreign bodies can be seen clearly in this MRI. One at the top of my brain, the other two behind each ear.

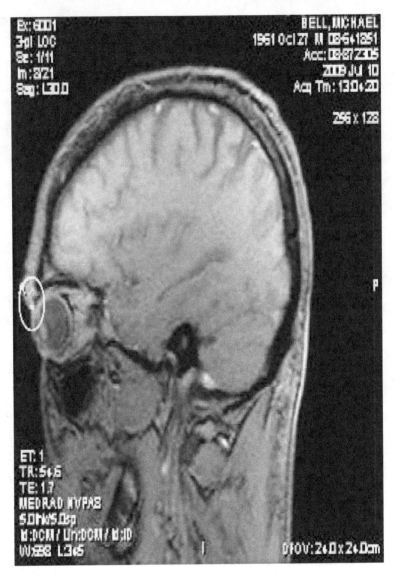

A foreign body can be seen in this MRI above my left eye.

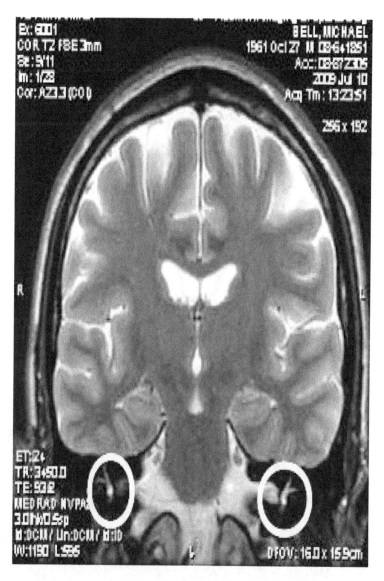

Two "rabbit ear" antenna devices can be seen below my brain.

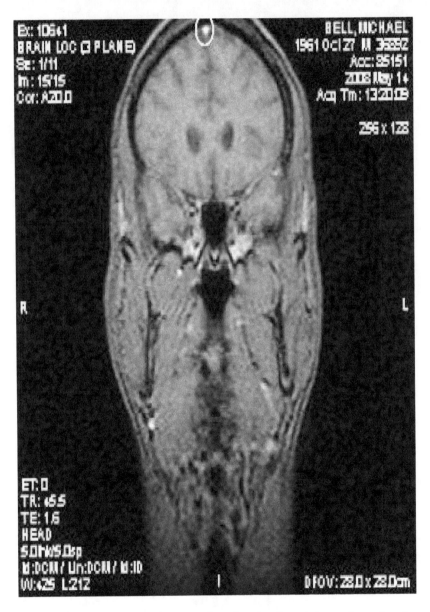

Another MRI image shows a foreign body on top of my brain.

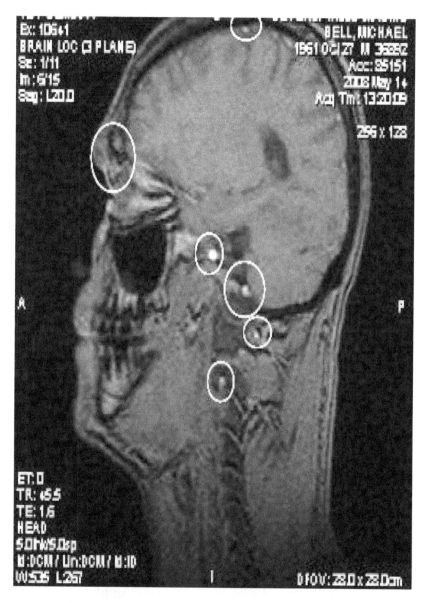

Six clearly visible foreign bodies can be seen in this MRI. One surgeon referred to these foreign bodies as "anomalies."

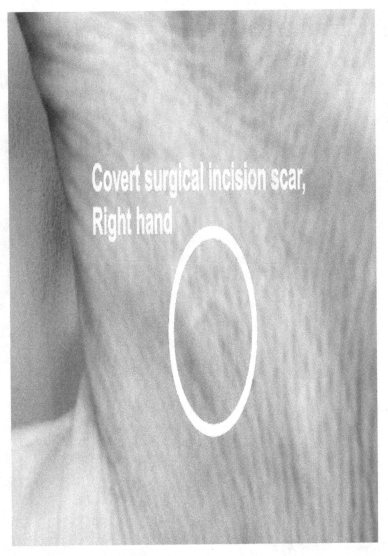

A foreign object can be seen. This object is located beneath a small surgical scar on my right hand.

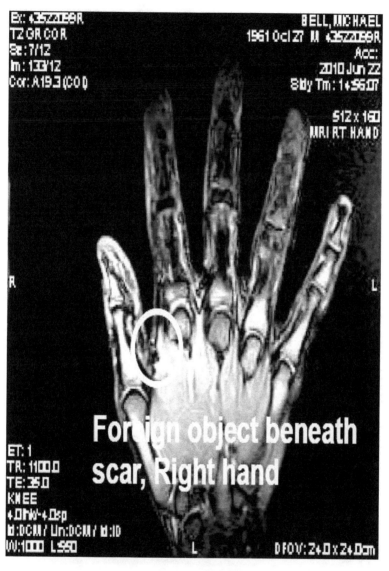

A foreign object can be seen in this MRI. This object is located beneath a small surgical scar on my right hand.

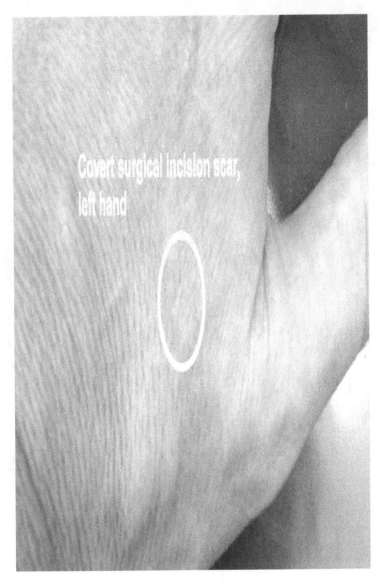

A cosmetic surgery scar on my left hand, directly above a foreign body

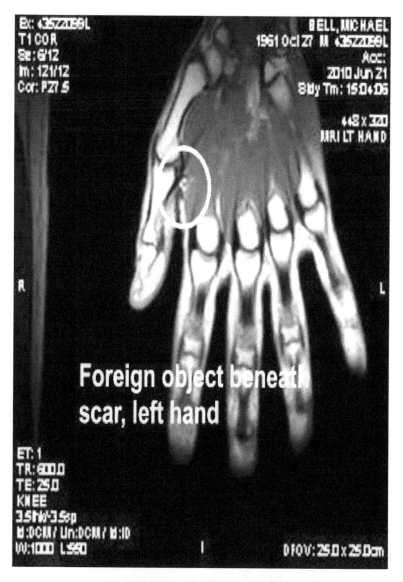

Foreign body shown in an MRI.

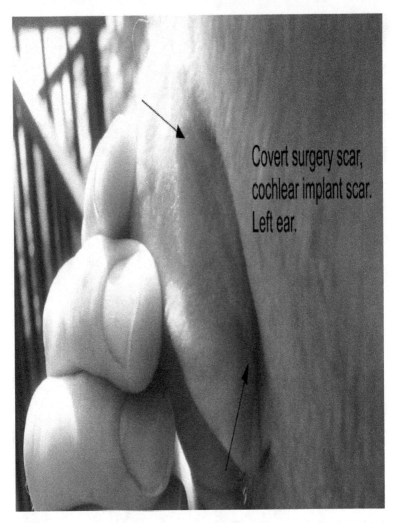

Covert surgery scar, cochlear implant scar. Left ear.

Fine, cosmetic surgery scars behind both left and right ears. These are not natural folds in the skin, but rather, evidence of covert cochlear implants.

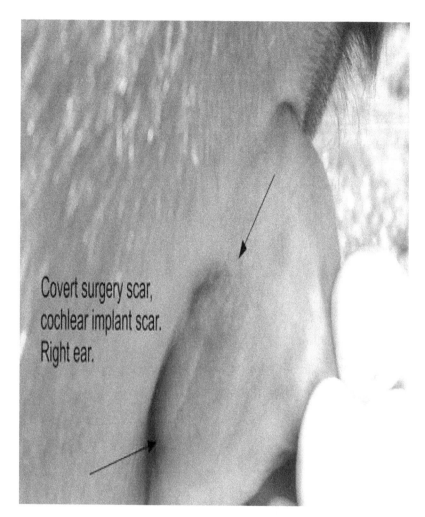

Covert surgery scar,
cochlear implant scar.
Right ear.

Fine, cosmetic surgery scars behind both left and right ears.
These are not natural folds in the skin, but rather, evidence of
covert cochlear implants.

❧ Chapter Eight ❧

Countermeasures: Shielding, Neodymium Magnets, Jammers, Tin Foil

"Thou dost frighten me with dreams and terrify me by visions."
Job 7:14

This chapter may be one of the most useful for Targeted Individuals. Countermeasures are not optional; they are necessary. Targets are most vulnerable when they are sleeping, so shielding of some form is essential. I will list some highly effective forms of active and passive shielding.

VCR Tape Shielding

This is easy to make, inexpensive, and highly effective in protecting the Target while he or she sleeps. Take a VCR tape and unscrew the four to six screws that are holding it together. Lay down long strips of packing tape with the sticky side facing up. Fold each end down, back onto the table or surface you are working on; this way the tape is held in place.

Next, remove the VCR tape from the open box and lay strips down which are the same length as the length of the tape. Be careful to line up the pieces of VCR tape in rows onto the sticky packing tape. Try to place each new strip of VCR tape as close as you can to the previous one, so you are almost doubling each layer.

At first this will seem tedious and tiresome, but soon you will become good at applying each new layer of VCR tape down next to the previous. Don't try to make a blanket all at once; instead, just keep applying narrow strips of VCR tape long enough to cover from below your chin all the way down to cover your feet. Then, start over and make another narrow strip. Cover each strip with another piece of packing tape, trapping the magnetic VCR tape in between the two.

Tape each complete strip to another one with more packing tape. Eventually, you will have enough stripes taped together to form a blanket. The blanket should be wide enough to cover your front side and wrap all the way around your body, whereas the two ends overlap and will be held in place by the weight of your body lying on them. Take care to confirm that plastic tape covers both sides of the blanket, which will ensure your skin will not come in direct contact with the VCR tape.

Also, hold the blanket up to a window. This will allow light through any places you may have missed. This passive form of shielding is effective because the VCR tape is magnetized and distorts and disrupts the frequency of the directed energy aimed at the Target.

111

It is also very important to have a T-shirt between you and this VCR shielding to absorb excess perspiration. Making a helmet using the same techniques mentioned above is highly recommended. Just remember to have space for your nose and mouth to be exposed for proper breathing. Again, if you decide to fashion a helmet, triple layer VCR tape is advised and also wrap a T-shirt or small towel around your head to absorb excess perspiration.

Neodymium Magnets

This is actually active shielding, as the magnetic force of these rare earth magnets is extremely strong, especially for such a small size. You can find rare earth or neodymium magnets available on many sites on the Internet. A good site that I like to use is called magnet4less.com. These magnets come in a variety of shapes, sizes, and purity levels. They are also used for pain and healing therapy.

Grade 52 is the highest, purest grade of neodymium magnets available to the general public. Grade 50 is probably the highest grade you will be able to find. These magnets are extremely strong and care must be exercised when using them, especially the higher pull-force models.

Each magnet has a North and South magnetic pole. When purchasing neodymium magnets, it is recommended to purchase an inexpensive pole detector meter, to remove the guesswork. Alternately, you can use a compass to find the true Northside of the magnet. By placing a compass on a table, slowly the true geographical Northside of the magnet will appear as the opposite of what the compass indicates. The Northside of the magnet is slightly stronger than the Southside, and is more effective at disrupting a frequency or signal aimed at a Victim through its extremely strong magnetic field.

Neodymium magnets will last up to four hundred years as long as they are not subjected to temperatures higher than one hundred seventy-five degrees. These magnets are extremely brittle and will chip or crack very easily if they are allowed to snap together or if they get dropped or banged around. Start small when getting use to carrying around these magnets. I would recommend buying between eight and twelve of the Grade 50 1" x 1/8"inch thick rare earth neodymium disc strong magnets with a pull force of 17.5 pounds.

Be very careful when first using these magnets, as they can pinch fingers and skin and can stick to metal surfaces, sometimes permanently. You may want to cover your magnets with some duct tape to protect them, as they are very brittle and will crack and chip easily.

You can carry a small group of these magnets in your pants pocket and may find that they offer a lot of relief from directed energy and implants. The magnetic field is so strong that it is able to disrupt an undesired frequency that is being aimed at you. Applying the magnets directly to an area of discomfort caused by directed energy or implants will provide instant relief. Just be careful not to leave these magnets too close to electrical equipment like computers or credit cards or any electronic device, as it may

113

damage these devices permanently.

Older implants may be permanently disabled by placing a neodymium magnet of perhaps a fifty pound pull force on top of the suspected area with tape for twenty-four to forty-eight hours. Some implants may take longer to disable. With brain implants and some newer implants it may not be possible to disable them. Neodymium magnets will, however, weaken any suspected implant and distort the frequency it gives off and the frequency it is receiving.

Jammers

Jammers are tricky—I can tell you from personal experience. If you get the right one, it may work very well for you—but only for a little while. Remember, whatever you do, your Perpetrators also know in real time what you are thinking.

Jammers are, for the most part, fairly expensive. It is easy to spend a lot of money on things that cannot be returned and do not help you at all. If possible, always try to buy from distributors that offer money back guarantees or unconditional guarantees.

Jammers come in a wide range of frequency ranges and are also used for different jamming purposes. Some jammers will block GPS tracking, if a transmitter is covertly installed on your vehicle. If you are dealing with implants, chances are the jammer you choose may work for a short time before your Perpetrators turn up the power of the attacks on you. Then, the jammer will only offer minimum protection.

The other problem with many jammers is that they are not always silent. This can draw unwanted and embarrassing attention to the user. Figuring out what frequencies you are jamming against is also difficult.

Still another problem with jammers is that they have a short battery life, even if rechargeable. You can spend a lot of money buying batteries that may only last less than one day. If you do your research or if you are scientifically gifted, you may find a jammer that works for you. However, I do not recommend them for all of the above reasons. Although new countermeasures are constantly being improved, the possibility of the perfect blocker or jammer still exists.

Tin Foil

Now you feel like you have completely gone bonkers by using tin foil to protect you from an unseen force. The truth is that tin foil can and does work. Sometimes, it is better than no shielding at all. However, it is a last resort when no other source of shielding is available. If you are using tin foil, always have something like a T-shirt or a small towel between your skin and the tin foil. You do not want direct exposure of your skin to the material. One problem with tin foil is that it can sometimes reflect the frequency that is emanating from you and it will end up bouncing back to you, in essence—slowly cooking you.

Emergency Blankets

These are similar to tin foil, but can be effective. Placing one emergency metallic blanket under your mattress and one on top of the top sheet or blanket on your bed will offer some relief.

Use Caution With All Shielding Methods and Techniques.

I am only advising the reader or Target of the methods that have worked for me. I had to spend a lot of money and thousands of hours of research to evaluate the effectiveness of the countermeasures that I have mentioned above. The user takes full responsibility for any methods or techniques I have shared. I will say that the Target must do *something*. Targeted Individuals must take responsibility and try to do something to protect themselves from the Perpetrators who have silently abused, tortured, and damaged their health.

Photographs of crude shielding, a helmet and blanket, fashioned from thousands of pieces of magnetic VCR tape. Also shown here is a four-hundred pull force neodymium magnet.

ᕲᕲ Chapter Nine ᕲᕲ

Digital Voice Recorders and Video Cameras: The Great Deterrents

"That which does not kill us makes us stronger."
Friedrich Nietzsche

Digital Voice Recorders

When you leave your residence, if you don't have a covert camera set up, a digital voice recorder will also provide evidence of a break-in should one occur. The best one on the market is a Sony made product and is very sensitive and powerful. It is even capable of recording voice to skull transmissions. Voice recognition technology is a very efficient form of evidence. Even if a voice is disguised, it can be decrypted by a specialist. I fully recommend purchasing a digital voice recorder; they are very inexpensive, even top of the line. The evidence could prove to be priceless.

The Invisible Crime - Michael F. Bell

Digital Video Cameras

One of the best pieces of advice I got from private detective and electronics expert, George Seymour when I visited him in Pocatello, Idaho, was to always carry a digital camera with me at all times. At first, I would take pictures of my Perpetrators sitting in their cars parked next to my car after they gave me the finger or honked their horns repeatedly at me.

Then, when I reported this behavior to the local police department in Columbus, North Carolina, they would always say the same thing: "Mr. Bell, that is just a picture of a man sitting in a pickup truck and that, is just a photo of a license plate. They don't prove anything."

I quickly realized the limitations of the digital camera. So I moved up to the next step—a digital video camera.

My current camera has an eight-hour filming capacity. The smaller the camera, the better, and rechargeable batteries are a must. Also, bring a freshly charged back-up battery in case of battery failure or for extended periods of filming. Even high-end digital video cameras are very plentiful and inexpensive these days. Let's face it: no one really enjoys being filmed, but only someone with something to hide will get angry when you film them. Perpetrators don't like video cameras because filming their behavior—such as flashing high-beam headlights, giving me the finger for no reason, or honking horns at me—actually now shows a pattern of behavior. This proves that these things I have been complaining about *really are* occurring and *really are* happening

119

to me.

The Perpetrators began to call the police and started complaining about my video camera filming, trying to get me into trouble with the authorities. One time, the police stopped me and questioned me. I told them that I was no different than the paparazzi: anyone out in public, in a public place, is fair game to have their pictures taken and/or filmed.

Now, anyone complaining about my digital video filming is suspect of being a Perpetrator as a matter of circumstance.

When asked, the local police respond to those people who complain about my filming with, "If you are out in public, Mr. Bell has the right to film anything he so desires; if you don't like it, stay at home or stay away from Mr. Bell." Sometimes just pointing the video camera at a suspected Perpetrator is enough to deter him or her from doing anything, even if the camera is actually turned off.

I fully recommend that any Targets should carry a digital video camera with them at all times. Any stalking that is witnessed by the Targets should be filmed and held for evidence. The key to the effectiveness of the video filming is constant, continuous filming, whether harassment is taking place or not. Targets must be proactive when videotaping.

Having the video camera visible will eliminate about ninety-five percent of public harassment. The smaller the camera, the easier it is to carry and put away in places where filming is prohibited such as any government building, post office, bank, or pharmacy.

When driving, both hands are on the steering wheel, but clutched in one hand is the live filming video camera which should be aimed at oncoming traffic traveling in the opposite direction. This will virtually eliminate all brighting or flashing lights at the Target's vehicle. The digital video camera should be resting firmly on top of the steering wheel, which provides smooth, clean filming and avoids shuffling or jerking the camera around.

When entering a public building, store, or office, the video camera must be turned off and the lens cap put back on. It is wise to tell the nearest employee that you have a video camera with you, but you are not filming in the store and that the camera is turned off. After a while, stores and banks which you frequent will become use to this seemingly strange filming behavior.

When asked why you have a digital camera and why they feel it necessary to film everything, the response should always be humble and answered, "For my own safety." When exiting a store, in the doorway, turn the video camera on again.

In addition to informing the store owners or managers, visit the local police station at least once to explain that you are being stalked and harassed. Tell them that private investigators said that filming what you see makes it easier to provide evidence that a criminal behavior pattern is occurring and that you are the Victim of ongoing, threatening, intimidating stalking and harassment.

A huge tip is for the Victim to make audible, verbal commentary from time to time while filming. Verbalizing what harassment you anticipate will virtually eliminate all public stalking and harassment. This behavior often involves spitting, menacing stares, mocking, taunting, laughing, flashing lights, honking, or giving the finger—all for no apparent reason.

Upon entering a parking lot while filming, sweep the parking lot by slowly driving around the parking lot or by covering the parking lot from one position and film the entire area. Commentary like, "Let's see what we have here today?" is highly effective to back up any predicted Perpetrator techniques and reveal them on film.

Another great tip to eliminate expected vandalism to your vehicle is to walk around the car and film the tires and the general appearance of the car before leaving it. This will eliminate slashed tires, key jobs, cracked windshields, and notes or messages left on the vehicle.

It may seem like a lot of work, but it is really very simple and easy to adjust to this new approach; it will become second nature to start filming. Insurance companies love digital footage, especially if a staged accident should occur.

Using the digital video camera beginner techniques will allow the Target to go out normally or do anything that they desire. As the Target becomes more proficient with the use of the video camera and the techniques mentioned in this book, they will start becoming more relaxed and feeling more confident.

Advanced techniques include setting up motion-activated covert or hidden digital video cameras or nanny cams around the

Victim's residence. A motion-activated or continuous-filming automobile covert camera, with infrared and night vision technology, is available and very useful for identifying the criminals that may vandalize your vehicle.

Perpetrators hate digital video cameras. Filming an intruder inside your residence, while you are away, will be undeniable evidence for any judge or police force. No longer must the Targeted Individual be isolated in their residence and feel frightened about a trip to the grocery store, post office, or the mall. Now, with the video camera, the Victim can take back their freedom, at least on one level.

There will always be the occasional harassment here and there, especially if you are in an environment where filming live is prohibited. The filming is so easy and so effective that things will start appearing to you as they did before the stalking and harassment began. You can casually drive around any suspicious, parked vehicle and discreetly film the license plate.

Many Perpetrators like to back their cars into parking spaces to hide their license plates from being filmed or written down. In these cases, you can simply walk around the parked vehicle while you are filming and pretend that you are just filming the area because it is such a beautiful day or perhaps you wanted to film the mountains or the forest or any excuse you can casually come up with.

The last tip for live, continuous videotaping is to be aggressive, but discreet, with the filming process. Being a covert and discreet video camera operator becomes an art. Targets using the above-mentioned beginner methods of filming for the first time will get guaranteed immediate and positive results.

If no stalking or harassing behavior is filmed, you can simply rewind the tape or erase the most recent film and simply tape over it. When arriving back home, remember to immediately plug in and recharge the camera for the next outing. As I stated, these are only beginner techniques.

Later, the Target will become proficient at filming and graduate to more advanced methods and techniques that I have developed, including on-board video cameras and covert camera techniques, which are also easy, inexpensive, practical, and highly effective. Button video cameras, sunglass, and visor video cameras are available in high definition all over the Internet, especially at spy shop websites, and are very inexpensive to purchase. Put these mentioned techniques to task and watch the instant, positive, desired results.

Any predicted behavior patterns caught on tape should be immediately reported to local police and/or saved for record— or better yet, posted on the Internet.

It is important for Targets who choose to start using a digital video camera to recover their freedom of movement, to remember the power of the video camera, and to respect it as one would anything that is used for protection purposes, such as a gun.

Just as it is against the law to brandish a firearm in some places, you must be respectful of the general public when using the constant, continuous filming technique. Following suspected Perpetrators or confronting them directly with a live-filming video camera is dangerous and should be avoided at all costs. It will inevitably end in an undesirable consequence. Seemingly casual, non-invasive, non-threatening filming is the goal.

Targets using videotaping as a form of evidence and protection from their predicament should aim to keep the filming process as covert and natural as to avoid negative attention. Blend in with the environment; don't be a *stand-out*. This is offered as practical advice to avoid ongoing, unpleasant situations and conditions.

✑ Chapter Ten ✑

Further Vigilance

"I am responsible for everything…except my very responsibility."
Jean-Paul Sarte

Essential Travel Tips Targets and Non-Targets

When traveling, especially via airplane, it is important to know and recognize these precautionary steps. These tips are also useful for anyone traveling anywhere—especially internationally. When packing your bag for domestic or international flights, always pack your clothing and anything you bring with you, yourself.

Carefully examine the empty baggage or luggage first, and check all pockets and zippered linings for anything that may be used to incriminate you: small packets of illegal drugs, bullets, small knives, or any form of weapon. Be wary of articles being introduced into your baggage. International travelers must keep a photo I.D. and passport with them at all times prior to travel.

Examine each and every piece of clothing, pockets and all toiletries, prescription medications, and vitamin containers thoroughly before departure. Once packed, this bag must be locked or zip-tied to prevent any potential corruption or contamination. It is easy for a criminal to set up a person by introducing anything illicit into their luggage or within the luggage linings.

Stalking Victims who have reported their victimization to local law enforcement are encouraged to make the airline aware of their situation. Harassment on airlines is prevalent. It's important to get the seat number of any perceived Perpetrator. Should any harassment occur, it's also important to discreetly make the supervising flight attendant aware of the situation and the suspect. These instances should be recorded since they could be vital evidence for the Target in possible future prosecution or in making a criminal claim. A small, pocket digital camera or cellphone with video/digital picture capabilities should be carried with the Target during travel.

As always, being prepared and proactive will help eliminate being the Victim of circumstance from occurring.

Preventing Intentional Covert Drugging

Products such as toothpaste, shampoo, and hand or body lotion, are often used for covert drug/poison application.

Methamphetamine or "Crystal Meth" is a cheap and popular drug choice for Perpetrators. It is usually colorless, odorless, and tasteless. Perpetrators may inject a dissolved, liquid form of this drug into a variety of food or toiletries. Even items such as doorknobs, toothbrushes, combs and hair brushes, can all be painted with Scopolamine or LSD-25, liquid Crystal Meth, and other drugs. Using this highly covert method of painting the drug directly onto a surface that the skin comes in contact with, it then becomes possible for trans-dermal absorption to occur. Crystal Methamphetamine, over time, is notorious for its destruction to teeth.

Rather than gamble in your absence from your residence, I recommend using a small backpack to carry all vitamins, prescription medications, and all toiletries with you when you leave home.

Yes, this is a burden, but think of the possible alternative. Being constantly, continuously drugged, may explain a number of nagging health issues such as insomnia, headaches, increased heart rate, tooth decay, skin rashes, and the feeling of being intoxicated for no apparent reason.

You must be proactive; nothing is out of the realm of possibility. Washing things like silverware and drinking glasses before use— even if they are alrcady clean—will then eliminate the possibility of covert drugging. Better safe than sorry is always important. Remember: If you can imagine something that can happen, do whatever you can to prevent that occurrence from happening.

Colorless, odorless, and tasteless, Scopolamine is slipped

into drinks and sprinkled onto food. Victims become so docile that they have been known to help thieves rob their homes and empty their bank accounts. Women have been drugged repeatedly over days and gang raped or rented out as prostitutes. In one case, a mother of three children was rendered so docile that she allowed her Attackers to take her youngest child.

Scopolamine not only blocks most memories from forming after it is given to the Victim, it can also block memories for up to several hours or even days before the drugging. Most troubling for police is the way the drug acts on the brain. Since Scopolamine usually completely blocks the formation of memories, unlike most date-rape drugs used in the United States and elsewhere, it is usually impossible for Victims to ever identify their Attackers. Only someone like me, with my photographic memory, would be able to stand a chance of remembering anything at all.

"When a patient (of U.S. date-rape drugs) is under hypnosis, he or she usually can recall what happened. But with Scopolamine, this isn't possible because the memory was never recorded," said Dr. Camilo Uribe, the world's leading expert on the drug. Scopolamine has an enduring and shady history in Colombia dating back to before the Spanish conquest. There are legends of Colombian Indian tribes that used Scopolamine to bury alive the wives and slaves of dead emperors and leaders to go to the afterlife with them. Finding the drug in Colombia these days is not difficult.

The tree from which Scopolamine is derived grows wild around the capital and is so famous in the countryside that mothers

129

warn their children not to fall asleep below its yellow and white flowers. The tree is popularly known as the *Boracherra (get-you-drunk)*, and the pollen alone is said to conjure up strange dreams. Statistics show that Scopolamine and Rohypnol are the two principle, recognized drugs used by criminals on their Victims in all abduction cases worldwide.

I can only warn you not to keep open food containers or beverages in your apartment. Do not leave half-finished bottles of water, Gatorade, wine, soda, or anything else in your residence. Thoroughly inspect plastic water bottle containers for punctures or needle marks before consumption. Initially, all abductions—especially involving women—are drugged through food or beverages. Victims can also be drugged through shampoo, toothpaste, hand lotion, cosmetics, vitamins, or prescription medications. Never leave food or drink unattended at a bar or restaurant; always finish everything you've ordered before leaving the table. Avoid "doggy bags" of unfinished food to take home, as one never knows what can happen to food once it's out of sight.

When I lived in Los Angeles, I was forced to *one-time* everything. That means if you don't finish a soda or food that is leftover in the refrigerator and you have to go out of the residence, the food that is open/ unsealed, should be thrown out or brought with you. Yes, it is wasteful and expensive to live like this, but now you have eliminated the possibility of being drugged through food or drink. The alternative—being drugged surreptitiously—is much more expensive and dangerous, by comparison. I am only sharing with you what you need to know to protect yourself.

ᐠᐟ Chapter Eleven ᐠᐟ

Medical Evidence

"His children are far from safety; They shall be crushed at the gate without a rescuer."
Job 5:4

The main problem with modern day medicine is that doctors are taught to think inside of a box. Anything outside of this box will not be recognized. Doctors are not familiar with the advancements in covert technology; therefore, they do not understand it or even believe that it's possible.

The big problem with doctors is that they were not schooled in the idea of thinking that the patient *may* actually be telling the truth.

Detecting and locating involuntary implants is not the job for a doctor; this is a job for an electronics expert or electrical technician. The only thing that doctors have to do with involuntary implants is that surgeons are the only ones qualified to remove them.

Ultrasound and MRI's are the only two tools available to detect and locate implants. It is not always easy to get a doctor to order an ultrasound or an MRI. Also, medical insurance companies don't like to pay for these tests because of their enormous expense. The other obstacle the Target faces is that even with an ultrasound and an MRI that clearly shows a foreign object, many doctors will not acknowledge them. It is even harder to find a surgeon willing to remove a foreign body. It is not unusual for a Target to get a positive ultrasound or MRI and continue to be passed from surgeon to surgeon—all unwilling to remove it. This can be expensive and frustrating.

I took all of my ultrasound images, MRI's, and photos—along with the doctors' reports—to the American embassy in the city of Madrid, Sprain. They could not help me, even with all of my evidence. The police were also unable to help me. If the Victim experiences stalking or electronic harassment while in another country, this makes the crime even more severe. It now becomes an international crime or can even be considered terrorism, because that is exactly what it is.

Sagitar could actually see and feel one of the implants above my eyes through the skin. He wanted to try to remove it himself. His assurance to me that he had one year of medical schooling under his belt was not exactly encouraging. We went to a large mall in the center of Madrid and bought everything necessary to make an extraction. Numbing gel, cotton pads, Lidocaine, Benzocaine, aloe wet-wiping pads, a small pair of scissors, tweezers, and the worst part of all—a box of razor blades.

132

The Invisible Crime - Michael F. Bell

We went back to the hostel where I was staying and set up two video cameras; then, we held that day's newspaper up to the camera to show what day it was. After a short introduction on what we were trying to accomplish, it was time for the surgery.

After about thirty minutes of numbing the area with Lidocaine and Benzocaine, Sagitar made a small, but painful cut above my right eyebrow, which I had just freshly shaved off for this highly irregular procedure. He could feel the implant, but because of all the scar tissue that had built up around it, he was not able to get a hold of it with the tweezers. He made another attempt, a second cut, slightly higher than the first cut; again, the scar tissue made it impossible for him to excise. So, we had to give up. Surprisingly, there was very little bleeding. I made sure to flush all of the evidence down the toilet, for fear of what the maid might think when finding blood-soaked cotton pads. He also tried a third cut on my chest, where there was a large bulge of scar tissue. Here, he continued to pull out scar tissue, but no implant.

Since we did not experience success during these attempts, I thought it would be smart to record over the video. Someone seeing such a video and not understanding the desperate circumstances surrounding it could possibly question my sanity. There was nothing wrong with me or my sanity. We had to try at least once—on our own—to get proof of my implants. The cuts were so small, that with the use of scar gel, they healed completely in less than two weeks. My trip to Madrid, Spain had provided me with doctor-acknowledged, demonstrative evidence of at least three foreign objects. My family doctor believed me and my most unusual story, but he could not find any surgeon to remove a single foreign body.

Although the technology that was implanted in me was high-tech, it was not without its flaws. Radio frequency (RF) meters for digital and analog signals are able to measure frequencies given off by implants. Older technologies are obviously easier to detect; conversely, the newer implant technologies are nearly impossible to detect.

Using something like an advanced Tektronix Spectrum Analyzer oscilloscope with the proper antenna, you would be able to capture the same information that the Perpetrators receive from their Victims. Using the proper equipment, my body would look like a human Christmas tree. Every implant could be seen, its exact location, at the exact depth in the skin; even the neural brain radio implants in my brain would all be easily seen. This is the same technology that the Perpetrators are using on me. This equipment is extremely expensive, even to rent. Most likely the frequencies being used on me are somewhere between 1MHz (megahertz) and 8 GHz (gigahertz). For the curiosity of the reader and for the benefit of the Target, I have included some general, common implant sites.

The tiny white, surgical scars that are the tell-tales of implants are usually symmetrical and corresponding to the same location on the opposite side of the body. One side will always be more pronounced and easier to find than the other.

Using a 5X mirror in one hand, standing in front of a well-lit bathroom mirror, you can examine the area behind each ear by pulling the ear forward with the free hand and holding the 5X mirror behind the ear. In the reflection, small vertical scars will be visible. They are sometimes hidden in the natural folds of the skin.

The navel is the most common area to be implanted, especially in women. Shave the area around the navel and then clean it out with a cotton swab dipped in rubbing alcohol. Usually vertical, although sometimes horizontal, a small white scar will be visible in the lower front of the navel or deep in the natural folds of the skin. It is much easier to find any scar if you are outside in natural light on a bright sunny morning. Look carefully and take your time. Some other areas to check include the inside and outside of each wrist and the base of the neck where it meets the chest. Within the eyebrows, a scar can often be found in the direction the hair is growing.

Perhaps the easiest location to find is in the gums of the Victim's mouth. Slide your finger along the lower gum line. At the base of what would be the lower canine tooth, you will feel what feels like a tiny BB or small bead floating within the gum line and not anchored. Implants in the upper gum line will be embedded and likely not felt by your finger. Peeling up the upper lip, small white scars may be visible at the root area of the upper teeth within the gum line.

Trackers or RF implants are often installed within the V between the thumb and forefinger. Please note, some scars will be single small straight lines, while others will be a tiny X or V shape. The inside and outside of the knees, the quadriceps, the calves,

135

ankles, backs of the arms and shoulders and the back of the neck, are all very common places to look for possible implant scars. Tiny white line scars can also be found on either side of the bridge of the nose.

If the implant was injected rather than installed, finding a scar will be extremely difficult and that type of implant is also likely to have migrated from the original point of insertion. Most of the time, there is a classic pattern where the implants are placed, which directly corresponds to specific nerve centers and main neural points throughout the body. If fully implanted, there will be tiny scars all over the Victim's body. Even if you locate the scar and a focal MRI shows a foreign, bright white object, it is often hard to find a surgeon willing to extract it.

White spots of hair, not to be confused with grey hair, on the top of the head are often an indication of the result of a neural transmitter that has been installed in the brain. Now, the hair which grows out of the scalp near the implant turns white. This can be accounted for, due to the constant, continuous low level microwave radiation exposure. This crime, at the very least can be referred to as illegal human experimentation.

Also, it is important to remember that someone who received an implant twenty years ago will have a different, more ancient form of this technology. For instance, older metallic implants can be seen clearly in X-rays. Older implants are also larger and easier to detect and remove. The smallest implant in the world today is manufactured by Hitachi and it is so small it is referred to as "powder." It is smaller than a common piece of sand.

There is another equally tiny implant called "microdust."

Implants can be introduced into the body while ingesting food. These are crystalline-designed implants that get trapped within the linings of the intestine, then scar tissue forms around them, securing them, holding them in place. Implants will either show up as bright white as in an MRI, and can also appear as a black, negative space or void. If you have a scar and have periods of missing time and a foreign object can be seen in an ultrasound or MRI, you may have an implant of some kind. The reason the scars on a Victim are so hard to find is because instead of stitches to close the point of installation or insertion, "Dermabond"—a kind of skin-friendly super-glue—is used. Scars are also cleverly hidden within wrinkles or natural folds of the skin.

The implants that were installed in me were *not* put in place by aliens: criminals are responsible for any implant that is within my body. Some Perpetrators, even shadow government groups, have been known to dress up in alien costumes or wear alien masks in order to further confuse and discredit the Victim. Today's implants will remain completely invisible in an X-ray or CT-scan. MRI and ultrasound are the only two methods of detection.

My Perpetrators wore a variety of different masks during all of my abductions, some vaguely resembling the typical alien being image, with large eyes and grey skin, but even though I was drugged, it was easy for me to see these were only costumes.

It must be noted at this time, that there are people who do suffer from severe delusional disorders, schizophrenia, and paranoia. Some of these people feel that they are being followed and monitored or watched through their television sets or sent subliminal messages over their car radios. This type of technology does exist, but to my knowledge is used on a very limited basis. There are people who are actually mentally unstable and imagine all sorts of unusual things. In reality, no one is really after them or is trying to undermine their lives. This is a mental state of dementia or delusion and is a product of a mentally ill person's imagination. Having scars and foreign objects throughout the body, in particular, neural foreign bodies are not a psychosis or the product of any imagination. My situation is very real. There are no issues here and nothing that can be blamed on something else.

Once a person is Targeted and fitted with implants, they are usually stuck in this situation for the rest of their lives. There are only two acknowledged cases of confirmed implant cases and removals. One is David Larson and the other is Robert Naeslund.

In February of 2010, I found an ear, nose, and throat doctor willing to remove one of the foreign bodies in my lower gum line in my mouth. He removed it, but refused to let me keep it; he said it had to go pathology and I never saw it again. I did get several good digital photographs of the foreign body and I have it pictured in this book. The doctor took out a nerve, some tissue, and the foreign body. This removal has left a portion of my chin numb to this day, but over time it should return to normal.

Photograph of an implant I had removed from the gum line of my left lower jaw. The doctor would not allow me to keep this object.

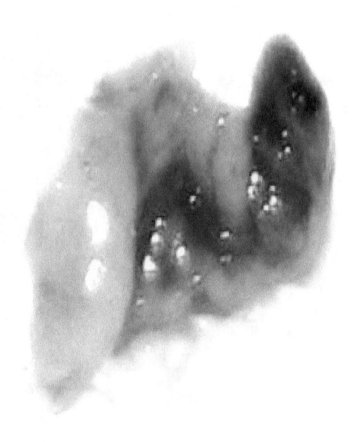

Another photograph of the same implant from a different angle.

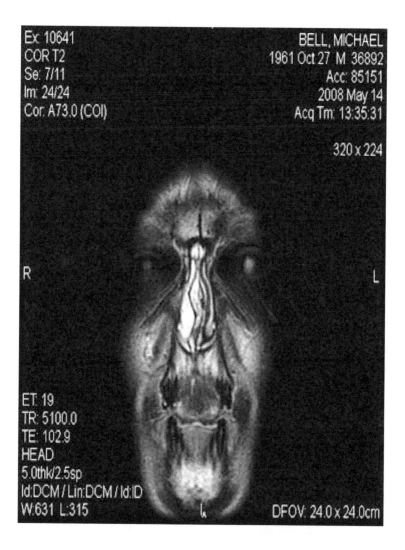

MRI of my face prior to the implant removal. The foreign objects are clearly visible on the lower jawline. Two white foreign bodies near the center of my chin, on either side.

Outside of being a Targeted Individual and being fully implanted with electronic transmission devices, I am a completely normal person, no different than your average, ordinary young man. I can remember some portions of the abductions better than others. Memory fragments and missing time were always consistent. I knew I had been drugged and something was being done to me, I just could not figure it out at that point. Later, the scars and the medical imaging would reveal my fate. No matter how hard my story may be to believe—it is, in fact, the truth.

None of the events or information mentioned in this book is fiction. It is all real life events that have since changed my life forever. This is a book of facts. These foreign bodies, clearly visible in my ultrasound and MRI images, are demonstrative evidence and are based in reality.

ᐸᔆ Chapter Twelve ᔆᐳ

Assembling Evidence and Proof to Make a Criminal Claim

"I smell blood and an era of prominent madmen."
WH Auden

In my endless visits seeking a surgeon to remove my foreign objects, there was one surgeon in Columbus, North Carolina who did admit to seeing many anomalies throughout my MRI images. He also said that unless he felt sure about what it may be, he would not just "cut [me] open and start digging around, looking for something." He had to be completely convinced there was something there.

Another problem the Victim of criminal implants will inevitably encounter is the question by the surgeon, "What do you think it is?" The Victim *cannot* mention the word microchip or implant, because most doctors either won't admit to the knowledge of such technology, or simply don't know that this type of technology actually exists—or worse, they will think that the

Victim is insane or mentally ill.

In the end of April 2010, I flew back to Madrid, Spain to see if I could find a surgeon there to remove my implanted foreign objects. At the airport Admiral's Club, a strange man approached me; as he walked past me, he grabbed my rear end with his hand. I took a still photo of him and reported this immediately to the airport security and they detained the man and gave him a citation.

At the Madrid Hospital, I had to pay 220 Euros for an evaluation. I showed the ophthalmologist my ultrasound images from July of 2009. When the ophthalmologist examined my eyebrows using a fluoroscope, similar to a live X-ray or ultrasound, he said to me, "You have what looks like two needles—one in each eyebrow— just above the eyes." I had to tell him that they may have been small pieces of a plastic fence that had fallen on me while in the barn at my parents' farm. This was a lie (a white lie), because if I told them that they were actually micro-transmission devices that were implanted in me, he would not have believed me.

The other thing I've encountered is that even if the doctors believe me, they are terrified into silence and will not help because they know how many atrocities that have been committed by the U.S. and other governments. Any implant that is not therapeutic and was installed without the Victim's knowledge or consent is obviously criminal. Many doctors do not want to help a Victim for fear that the Perpetrators will harm them or their families; therefore, they do not want to get involved.

On this visit to Spain, the doctor said that I could have the foreign objects above my eyes removed, but not until two months later. I did not want to stay in Spain for more months of waiting or fly back again in two months.

I thought I was being harassed by a passing car that seemed to flash their lights at me. Sagitar said it appeared they were flashing their lights because they had just come over a hill. We got into an argument and I ended up leaving his house as a guest of his family and I was forced to stay in a hostel closer to the airport. I ended up leaving Madrid by myself, with really nothing accomplished on this trip. It was a very expensive disappointment.

I found another doctor in London, England, who was willing to re-ultrasound the foreign object in my navel. I told him I had a scar in my navel and this object, which had shown up in previous ultrasound and MRI images, was causing me great pain. He agreed to a consultation and also agreed to evaluate the ultrasound for my "small lump" which was causing me discomfort. He said he could not promise the excision, but based on what I had told him, the chances were good that he may be able to have the navel's foreign body excised. This time, I told the doctor I really didn't know what the foreign object could be.

This was the truth, because until a suspected implant is extracted from someone and it is acknowledged— and it is actually sitting there on the table—who really knows what it is?

The consultation fee alone was 350 English pounds or around $500 U.S. dollars. The ultrasound would be 328 English pounds or around $450 U.S. dollars. This is very expensive, not to mention the expense of the airplane round trip ticket and a week in a hotel and other related expenses; I felt it was something I had to do. I had to try. If I don't try, I lose automatically.

Also, at this point, I had been living with my mother and father at their house, for over a year-and-a-half. No man who is forty-eight years old wants to live with his mommy and daddy, but these were extraordinary circumstances, and they had been tolerant of me. They had encouraged me to get a place of my own, but I was afraid that the druggings, poisonings, and break-ins would start occurring again.

The room where I was staying in my parents' house had been broken into several times during my stay there. There were signs that Perpetrators had access, signs such as the plastic shower curtain being repeatedly torn and punctured.

Never allowing the Targeted Individual to feel safe and secure is a stronghold of organized stalking and harassment. Making the Victim feel like there are no safe zones is psychologically damaging as well as just plain frightening and scary.

Although I could not prove it, I was sure that at least some, if not all, of the eight employees working at my parents' house had some hand in a portion of my stalking and harassment. Who else would have been able to gain entrance to my room and know exactly when I or my parents were away? How could someone in broad daylight get past these employees and get into the house without them noticing? It just is not possible. This strong sense of suspicion would have to wait to be proven later.

I felt a certain amount of safety living at my parents' house, although I continued to receive directed energy or microwave burns on my body, and continued to suffer sleep deprivation and frightening and bizarre, manipulated, vivid dreams.

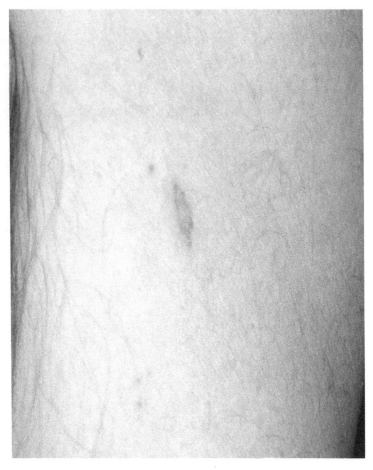

This is a photograph of a directed energy/microwave burn on my upper forearm.

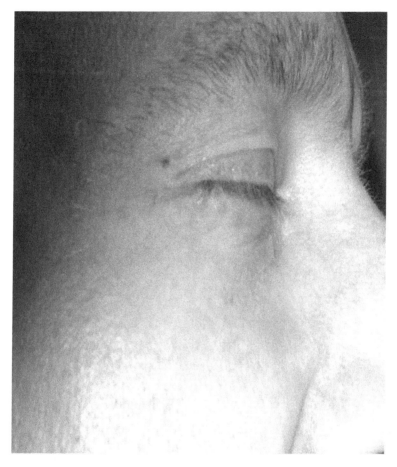

The photograph below shows burns to my upper and lower left eyelids of my right eye.

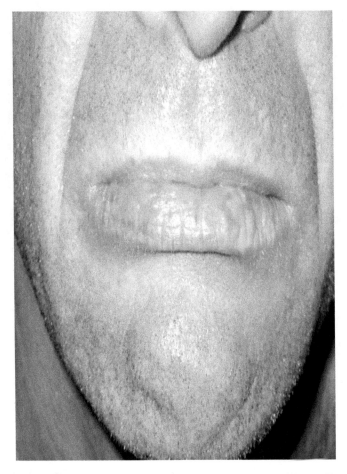

This photo shows evidence of burns on my lower lip.

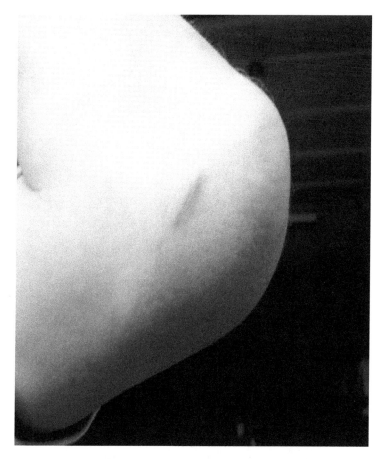

A linear burn on my left elbow.

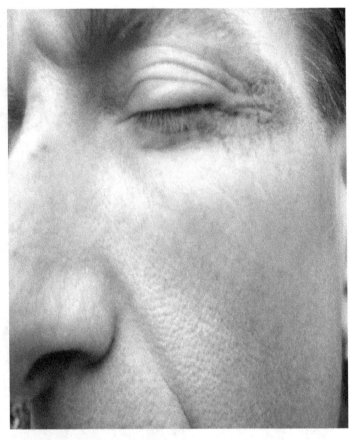

A severe, third degree directed-energy microwave burn to the upper and lower eyelids of my left eye and the surrounding area.

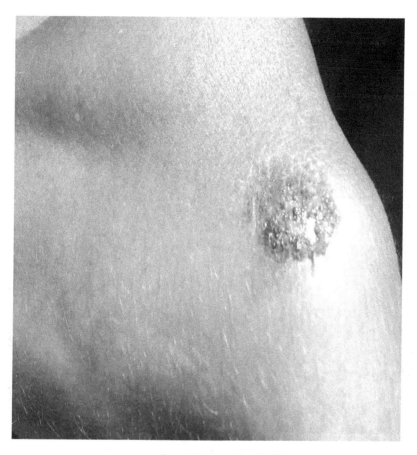

A severe burn to my left elbow.

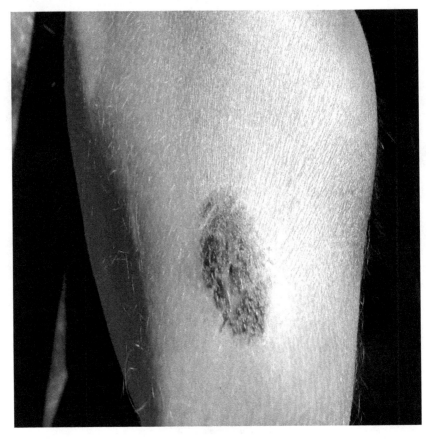

A severe burn to my left elbow from a different angle.

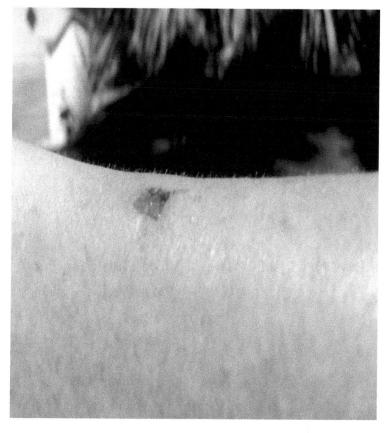

A square-shaped burn to left forearm.

☙ Chapter Thirteen ❧

Don't Forget to Tell Everyone

*"And now there is merely silence, silence, silence, saying all we
did not know."*
William Rose Benet

If you are a Targeted Individual, your family will soon
tire of hearing about the stalking or complaining about
the ongoing harassment. It is important to use the phrase
"organized stalking" rather than "gang stalking." It sounds more
credible, and even mentioning the word gang, gets people thinking
of graffiti, drug dealers, prostitution, and extortion. Although these
crimes may be linked to the organized stalking, using the word
"organized" will ultimately be more helpful.

You are encouraged to do as much research on the subject
as possible. Telling all of your family and friends, and using the
right presentation, will increase your credibility. When discussing

this crime with non-Targets, remember that you are going to face a tough time convincing others that you are a Victim of anything or any crime at all.

If you suspect that you have been drugged or poisoned, it is important to get a blood toxicology report immediately. Most date rape or abduction drugs leave the system very quickly. If abducted and drugged, just tell the staff at the local emergency room that you think somebody may have slipped something into your drink or your food. Telling stories about abductions like the story and account I have shared with you will not help you at all.

Later, after a drug screening shows a drug present in your blood and/or after an implant is removed, you may tell the whole truth, no matter how unusual it may be. Then, you will have undeniable evidence to back up your story.

Remember, also, that this crime is designed to make you sound crazy or like you have lost your mind. This is what makes this invisible crime perhaps the most perfect and ingenious one.

When you present your case or any aspect of it to the local police, you must remain calm at all times, no matter how frightened you may be. Speak slowly, without panic—and without using hand gestures, while describing what has happened to you. Using devices like the Sony Digital Voice Recorder or an RF digital or analog frequency meter will also add evidence to the crime that is being committed.

I can tell you from personal experience that this crime is a living nightmare for the Targeted Individual. You must remain strong, drink lots of water, and take lots of vitamins. Vitamin and water intake may be two of the most important pieces of advice for survival. The constant exposure to microwave energy will slowly break down your immune system, speeding up the deterioration process. Eating well, exercising, staying focused, and retaining a positive attitude will make all the difference. Citrus fruit juice such as grapefruit, orange, or lemon juice are highly acidic and will help the body slowly break down any foreign bodies such as illegal microchip implants. Of course, this information is good advice for everyone anyway, but it is critical for anyone who is a Target.

It is easy to let being a Target get your spirits down. That is what the Perpetrators want. That's what they are counting on. Just remember: whatever makes a Perpetrator happy is going to be bad for the Target. Conversely, living your life, going out, seeing friends—and, most of all, laughing—will make the Perpetrators mad. Laughter really is the best medicine. Having a good sense of humor—though difficult at times—will get you through the toughest of times. Attitude is everything.

You should try not to allow yourself to become isolated, as that is also another goal of the Perpetrators. Targets have to use a kind of mental anesthesia, exactly like a soldier does. In order to succeed, you must, on some level, consider yourself already dead; that way, you have nothing left to lose and you become less afraid of the unknown and the unpredictable.

⨏ Chapter Fourteen ⨏

Resolution and the Road to Freedom

"*Once you eliminate the impossible, whatever remains, no matter how improbable, must be the truth.*"
Sherlock Holmes (by Sir Arthur Conan Doyle, 1859-1930)

I should mention that this true story never flowed like a movie. At many points I was stopped, not knowing what to do next. Many times, I had to wait for the next step, whatever it was. Traveling to Europe was not only expensive, it was always a gamble. Since nobody helped me, I tried to do the best to help myself and at the least, obtain credibility.

This is not an easy story to believe. It was created by the design of the Perpetrators. It is what the Perpetrators have built into the crime itself by creating the perfect crime that no person will believe is possible. Ask any Target; nobody believes him or her. It's uphill the whole way. However, persistence always wins.

Organized stalking involves total strangers harassing total strangers. Targets never know who is there to harass them. This cannot help but make them fearful of everyone, to some degree. There is nothing Targets can do besides video filming to protect themselves. The Perpetrators would like nothing more than have the Targets get frustrated and act out. In the end, it will be the Targets getting hurt either by incarceration or being institutionalized.

As I counted down the days to my trip to London, I also noticed that my Perpetrators were tightening the screws, turning up the harassment level. A simple trip to the store became a major project. I had to bring the video camera and leave a camera or digital recorder running in my apartment while I was gone. There were many days when I would go hungry instead of driving to the supermarket or a restaurant.

Since becoming a Targeted Individual, I was no longer able to work. I couldn't sleep, so that made driving to work and maintaining a productive work day impossible. My social life, although I was always slightly reclusive, was now non-existent. Imagine trying to go out on a date and then explaining to the girl that you can't work because people are constantly following you and intimidating you or that you have biomedical implants throughout your entire body. You can't tell people that are non-Targets; they just don't understand. It is a terrible cycle of torture and helplessness.

My trip to London resulted in new ultrasound scans and an additional findings report from my radiologist, Dr. George Raja. I may note at this time, Dr. Raja found the foreign object in my navel immediately and although he did not include it in his report, he acknowledged two identical foreign objects within each eyebrow. The report review follows:

Dr. "G"
Harley Street
London, England
12 June 2010
Medical Report
Re: Mr. Michael Bell d.o.b. 27/10/1961

I reviewed Michael Bell in my consulting rooms at the London Clinic on the 11th June 2010. As described in my previous letter, he is extremely concerned about the development of linear scars bilaterally above the eyes, behind his ears and also within the navel region. I am afraid I am at a loss to explain these abnormalities but he clearly finds these most distressing. My radiologist at the London Clinic, Dr. "R," spent some considerable time with Michael Bell, first of all reviewing the imaging that he had already undertaken in the United States. He also performed a detailed ultrasound assessment of the abnormal areas. He described that within the subcutaneous tissues of the superior navel region there was a linear highly reflective structure seen. This measured approximately 5 mm in length and less than 1 mm in thickness. It lies 6 mm below the skin. The radiologist noted that this had already been investigated elsewhere. He was uncertain as to the nature of this structure. There were a number of possibilities. First it could represent some thickened fascia or fibrous tissue, second he could not exclude a small foreign body but he did think this was less likely.

Mr. Bell is clearly symptomatic, particularly with regards to the abnormal area in the navel region. I have told him that I am not sure whether a surgeon would attempt to excise the abnormal area seen and I would be worried that in the process it could cause more pain rather than less. It seems that he is willing to take this risk as for him it would be important to confirm or refute whether or not there is a problem there. I don't think that any further imaging in London is likely to shed any further light on this matter and I hope that he is able to use this information to get some answers which I am sorry that I've been unable to provide for him in any more detail.

> *Yours sincerely,*
> *Dr. "G"*
> *Consultant General Physician*

This comment came from a legal observation of my ultrasound analysis and findings.

What I find bizarre is that the examining physician thinks that removing an object that is a mere 5 mm by 1 mm, which is a mere 6 mm beneath the skin, might cause more pain than I might want to have to suffer.

How does this doctor explain this bizarre assessment? If it were a cancerous tumor, would the same assessment be made? 'Uh-oh. Leave it there. Removing it might be painful.'

And no recommended biopsy? I think this requires an explanation.

"J"

The doctor responded to this comment in the following

letter:

> *Dear Mr. Bell,*
>
> *Thank you for your email.*
>
> *My professional opinion remains that the ultrasound abnormality does not warrant a biopsy. The appearances on ultrasound suggest that in the superior navel region, the reflective structure most likely represents thickened fascia or fibrous tissue. The radiologist stated in his report that a small foreign body could not be excluded, but this was thought less likely. However, my understanding was that you were planning to consult with a surgeon on your return to the US to discuss the results of our imaging. There is no question of this being a 'cancerous tumour' and therefore it is not appropriate for a lawyer to trivialise your problems in the manner implied in the email below.*
>
> *I am sorry if you are in any way dissatisfied with the outcome of our consultation and it may be helpful for you to seek a second opinion from a physician in the United States.*
>
> *Yours sincerely,*
>
> *Dr. "G"*

Often times, doctors are either in on this massive abuse and are able to deny the existence of any foreign body or the Perpetrators made contact with the doctor and threatened him or told him misinformation about the patient. Victims of implants will find it difficult to find a surgeon, let alone finding a doctor to give an honest, concerned examination and consideration.

Now, I was completely on my own in my little apartment. I had to leave a live running video camera and the use of a concealed digital voice recorder each time I left the residence. Each night when I went to sleep, I had to barricade my door with a large sofa and a few chairs. I had to leave things in certain locations like a table in front of the refrigerator, just to make sure the small amounts of food I had were not corrupted or tainted in any way.

Additional MRI images I got from different imaging centers were often out of focus or the picture ended just where an implant site was located.

I had even reached out to the famous Dr. Roger Leir, known for his "Alien" implant removals. I sent acknowledged radiology reports, as well as several dozen images all showing, the bright white, dense foreign objects. He never replied back to me.

Another important thing for a Victim to remember when dealing with doctors: the less said, the better. Never use the words implant, microchip, or biochip. You may get sent to the psychiatric unit for evaluation. I was sent to three different psychiatric wards in Los Angeles in just an eight month period. Each time, they released me, finding nothing wrong with me.

Cedars-Sinai Hospital tried to bill me $26,000 for a six-day stay at one of their observation units. I had to fight that bill for over a year until they decided not to charge me. I was also sent to Del Amo Hospital in Torrance, California to be evaluated after an individual in a van threw a cinder block wrapped in plastic at my car and broke all the windows on the passenger side. The impact of the block also deployed the airbags.

There are many side effects or capabilities that implants can perform, one of which is making the Victim's skin feel as though bugs are crawling on it or the feeling of being bit by a small, unseen insect. When I complained about this unpleasant condition to the doctors at UCLA Medical Center, they locked me up for fifteen days.

Just prior to getting to the hospital, I was covertly drugged again with what I believe was, again, Scopolamine or Rohypnol. This dosage of the drug given to me made me act irrational and it took several days for the full effects to wear off. When I tried to explain to the doctor assigned to me that I had been drugged, he refused to believe me.

I had been taking an anti-parasite medicine called Ivermectin to stop what I thought were skin parasites that I had been infected with on a recent trip to Mexico to climb some very high-altitude volcanoes. The doctor wrongly diagnosed that I had overdosed on the Ivermectin.

This is impossible. I actually called the manufacturer of Ivermectin, a company called Merial. The customer service representative said he had never heard of anyone ever having hallucinations or overdosing on this anti-parasitic drug. I had to use the version of this medication that is normally used on swine and cattle, which cost $130 for a three-month supply. The human version of the exact same medication cost nearly $1,000 for a one-month supply.

Living by myself again was nice in some respects. No one—especially a single young man of forty-eight years—wants to live with his parents. Being a Victim of organized stalking, electronic harassment, and mind control can ruin all of the Victim's relationships—even with family.

Forget about dating; no young lady would believe the Victim's story—and if she did, she would not want to get involved with the Victim for fear of becoming a Targeted Individual herself. This is often the case. Girlfriends of the Target are often drugged, raped, and abused.

The Perpetrators are so well organized and so sly, this may happen without the girlfriend ever being aware of it. Small, but noticeable, property damage may also occur. Phone calls in the middle of the night with no one on the other end or frequent wrong number calls are earmarks of the Perpetrators. New Victims are not aware that the bright lights of an oncoming car traveling in the opposite direction or the honking horns of passing cars are signs that the harassment has begun.

I purchased a Kodak Zi8 Pocket HD Digital Camcorder, the same size as a BlackBerry. With this camera, I was able to go everywhere and film covertly without drawing attention to myself. I don't recommend the use of a video camera with the tell-tale swing out screen to anyone who plans on using the footage at a later time to prove harassment. This type of camera could get you into trouble, from either an angry Perpetrator or anyone who does not want to be filmed. Even though it is your right to film anything or anyone you want out in a public place, some people don't care about that right; they could either smash your camera or break your nose. No, they are not allowed to do this and will probably have to go to jail for this assault; however, it may be too late after the damage has been done. *Keep it simple to be safe.*

In the future, all cars will have cameras in them. It will cut down on random vandalism and insurance company costs. If a car with a camera installed in it gets into an accident, the video will show everything. The car's speed and position on the road ultimately will prove, without a doubt, which driver is at fault.

On June 22nd, 2010, I had MRI's of both hands and wrists. Bright white spots showed up directly beneath scars I still have on my hands and wrists. The radiologist made no mention of these anomalies in his report.

On the night of July 23, 2010, I was staying for two nights at a small cottage in the backwoods country of Tryon, North Carolina. Although I now had my own apartment, the landlady who rented the apartment needed to use it for two days to display photographs taken by her boyfriend, a local photographer. She went out of her way to find a place for me to stay for the two-day event.

That night, I went to sleep at approximately 8:00 p.m. I woke up at about 3:00 a.m. drugged on something and my rear end hurt like hell. Also, I noticed there was some kind of dark green lubricant smeared onto the tissue paper when I wiped my buttocks.

I was still half-drugged and could not risk driving. The next morning, I woke at about 7:30 a.m., half-remembering the events of just hours before. I took a shower and moved my bowels as usual.

In retrospect, I should have just gone straight to the police or the hospital for an examination, not only to prove that I had been raped, but to take a blood test to show the evidence that I had indeed been drugged.

When I had gone to sleep the night before, I placed all of my financial reports and bank statements beside the bed next to me. I had intended to destroy these extra documents at my parents' house the next morning by burning them in the fireplace. I could not simply throw out documents that contained valuable financial information like bank statements or credit card bills, because they could be stolen and accounts could be cleaned out.

When I got up that morning, the documents were missing, along with a bottle of shampoo. I later found the documents strewn around the front porch of the cabin as well as the missing bottle of shampoo. I went straight to the emergency room after informing the local police what had happened to me. I spent the better part of five hours getting rape-kit tested at the hospital and filling out police reports.

For the next three weeks after the drugging and rape, my face had a red rash, especially under each eye, and I had a breakout of small cysts and pimples. This was the result of my body getting rid of the toxins released during the drugging.

The Invisible Crime - Michael F. Bell

On August 9th, 2010, I had a removal surgery for the foreign object in my navel at North Central Baptist Hospital in San Antonio, Texas. The surgeon, whom I will refer to as "Dr. S," originally said he would remove my foreign object. He referred to it as a small node. He chose to cut a small incision, closed the incision, and left the foreign object inside of me. So, nothing was accomplished on this trip; I was the same. It would have been no different than if I had not gone at all.

My guess is that the Perpetrators got to him and threatened that if he removed the foreign object and allowed me to keep it as proof, they would retaliate in some way. This happens to almost all other Victims. If it were a piece of glass or wood, a stone, or a piece of metal, any surgeon would most likely remove it, especially if it was causing the person pain and interfering with his sleep.

I have included in this book the original ultrasound reports and images and my original MRI images. All of the radiologists who viewed my MRI images refused to acknowledge the foreign objects or anomalies that can all be easily seen, even by someone who is not a radiologist. I have also included photographs of some of the nearly two-hundred small surgical scars that cover my body from head-to-toe, actual X-rays, medical photos, and records.

I have also included two photographs of the one implant that was removed from my gum line in my lower jaw. The doctor refused to let me keep it. Pathology described it as a "mucoid formation." I have included the original MRI, clearly showing four dense, bright white objects in my lower jaw—all symmetrically placed and all exactly the same size.

Pictures are important.

The book also contains photographs of actual pictures of non-therapeutic, GPS tracking, and torture devices which are available for purchase by anyone on the Internet. They are known as "psychotronic weaponry," combining the words psychological and electronic. Just go on the Internet and search organized stalking, electronic harassment, and mind control. There are literally thousands of links and websites dedicated to this invisible crime. All of the weapons, diagrams, and technology are legally available for sale on the Internet.

I have also included photographs of my own personal microwave burns on my body. These burns are unique in their appearance, unlike a typical burn that comes from an external heat source like a curling iron or an open flame, which blister immediately. Microwave burns originate from the inside out. At first, what appears to be a small scratch starts to grow larger over a period of days; then, a purple blister appears on the skin approximately a week later. It is exactly the opposite of an external burn. It takes about six months to a year for the scar to disappear.

I have been to over thirty surgeons around the world, none of whom would remove any of my foreign objects. I continue to be attacked and stalked wherever I go, even in other countries and other states. The Perpetrators still break into my apartment; small, but noticeable, damage occurs on a regular basis to my personal property including my vehicle and my clothing. Using my video camera wherever I go has cut down on a lot of the harassment, but it still happens.

This account of my isolated situation is one-hundred percent true. My experiences mirror exactly the same organized stalking, electronic harassment, and mind control techniques used on thousands of other American citizens and people around the world.

My hope in writing this book is to make the American public aware of these atrocities and stop this complete invasion of privacy and sullying the images of innocent Victims, all of whom have done nothing to deserve this cruel and inhumane mistreatment.

This technology was originally perfected by the United States government. I believe this information was either sold or stolen—or both—to criminal organizations who are in control of it to this very day.

Because no one explains what or why this is happening to the Victim and because the organized stalking is done by complete strangers, to complete strangers, Victims tend to mistrust people in general and often become isolated, frustrated, and severely depressed. I remain hopeful and optimistic, despite determined efforts to destroy me both mentally and physically.

ᑯᕊ Chapter Fifteen ᕉᕋ

Moving On and Getting Back on Track

"This generation is a wicked generation; it seeks for a sign, and yet none shall be given to it."
Luke 11:29

Although I was no longer living under the relative safety of my parents' home, my small apartment in the town of Lynn, North Carolina, was not really living as I had known it.

After being spoiled with the everlasting sunny days and pleasant nights of living in Los Angeles, life anywhere else could not compare. I was simply existing in North Carolina, not actually living. Surviving, not enjoying life for all it had to offer.

In the last week of October 2010, I traveled to see an old friend in Burlingame, California, the first time I had returned to the state of California since my crime had forced me to leave. There, I bought a book in an obscure little bookstore; a book which would later inspire me to want to live again. The book, Laird Hamilton's

172

"Force of Nature: Mind, Body, Soul (And, of Course, Surfing)". In all honesty, it was this book that gave me back the zest for living. Adventure and seeking out the great unknown, and living with a purpose have become my goal.

Two weeks later, in November of 2010, I booked a flight to Maui, Hawaii, staying for five nights at the Four Seasons Hotel in Wailea. Despite informing the extremely tight hotel security force of my presence, my privacy was compromised. Although subtle, I was harassed by the local chapter of criminals. On the second day, somehow my room security was breached and a brand new pair of swim trunks had a pocket cut out. Most people would not be aware of this small, but noticeable, form of intimidation; I was all too familiar with it. Walks on the beach would result in crossings of seemingly other tourists, always cutting me off or walking into me. Yes, sometimes in a crowded destination like Hawaii people will end up doing things at the exact same time: common coincidences. If "coincidences" constantly occur, they are no longer just mere coincidences and the word coincidence has lost all context and definition.

Because I woke up early, being on East Coast Time, I would receive minimal interaction with other guests. Crime is a major problem everywhere, and Hawaii has more than its share. A constant guard must be upheld by all who travel. There is no such thing as being too prepared or organized. Small occurrences, such as opening my hotel room door and walking down the corridor, would result in half a dozen other guests arriving or leaving their rooms at the split second I opened my door or returned to my room, no matter what time of day or night. Although some of these encounters could be written off as pure chance, not all. My third day involved being rather clumsily followed around the hotel premises by an Afro-American, forty-something male, constantly communicating via a cell phone with a Bluetooth earpiece. I actually snapped his picture and confronted hotel security about him; they were unaware of his presence and he quickly disappeared. I am aware of the difference between paranoia and real concern, and sometimes it is a blurry line separating the two. The goal of the criminals is to make the Targeted Individual suspicious of everyone. To become sensitized to all stimuli, sight—sound, smell, taste, even sleep—can be very overwhelming to new Targets. Imagine the fright and horror of going to sleep at night, when one is most vulnerable, and having your dreams manipulated. It does happen, whether you choose to believe it or not. The truth cannot be disputed.

I met with the Chief of Security upon my arrival at the hotel and completely informed them of my situation; it was not foreign to them. I explained to him that I was a Victim of organized stalking and he told me he was familiar with the situation, and went as far as to tell me that sometimes the government is involved.

To travel as a Target is a huge endeavor. Airports, taxi cabs, restaurants, and stores are all areas where the Victim will inevitably be exposed to a new group of Perpetrators, all complete strangers. Changing one's daily routine is necessary and recommended. Vacations are no longer the luxury they were before becoming a Target—they can turn into living, breathing nightmares. Cornering the Target becomes easy for Perpetrators, particularly in elevators. Avoiding unnecessary eye contact with other people becomes habit. Never let your guard down; this is good advice whether you are a Target or not.

To be safe and not have your possessions corrupted or compromised, I would avoid having the housekeeping staff clean your room.

If one is on a trip for a week or less, this is normal and easy to do. Longer trips would require the Victim to be present during the changing of sheets and towels, and the general cleaning of the room. Being in the room will also speed up the process and one can then put the "Do Not Disturb" sign on the door and not remove it until the day of departure. Informing the front desk that you do not wish to have anyone enter your room will increase your privacy as well as safeguard your room from possible corruption.

Once all the precautions have been taken, now the Target can try to enjoy the vacation, relax, and smile. It is far too easy to become bitter, reclusive, and isolated. Don't ever turn your back on your food, drink, or your personal possessions. There are many "sharks" and people who will wait for just the right time to grab your wallet or purse the moment you go for a swim or use the restroom. This is the world we all live in today; it can happen, and you must prevent the possible from happening. Even though it may be a vacation, it is not recommended to consume excessive amounts of alcohol.

No matter what length the Victim goes to achieve a harassment-free atmosphere, there will be small encounters from random Perpetrators; it's simply unavoidable. If intimidation is experienced, tolerate it. Don't let the Perpetrators win. Stay focused, but don't ruin your trip with paranoia or delusion. This is easier said than done. The longer one has been a Target, the less the distractions will be bothersome. The more tolerant the Victim, the more frustrated the criminals will become. Things like stepping on your foot or bumping into your chair at a restaurant happens to everyone, but for the Target it will become increasingly clear that these small "accidents" are intentional. Don't react to these situations; instead, try to become blind to them. Taking this attitude is all one can do to preserve one's sanity.

Restaurants, particularly when traveling alone, should be approached earlier, when they open, avoiding the "crunch" or the most crowded times. The beach is a place where it is very simple for criminals to attack. Loud talking, humming, whistling, or singing to themselves is a tactic Perpetrators use to annoy the Victim. Kicking sand onto your towel or dripping water on you as they pass by can be expected, so don't be surprised or frightened. Perpetrators are bullies. Just suck it up and ignore it. It really is true; ignorance is bliss. When using public transportation, especially on the day of departure, use a taxi service the hotel recommends. This is especially important when traveling internationally. Go to sleep early and arise early. Most importantly, actually enjoy your vacation; don't let it make you feel like a prisoner counting the days until you leave.

The Invisible Crime - Michael F. Bell

My trip to Hawaii was enjoyable; the soft warm breeze, pleasant aroma of native flowers, and of course the classic Mai Tai with muddled mint. I used the same taxicab driver for both my arrival and departure, setting up the future pickup upon arrival. Safety is insured with organization and confidence. My confrontations were rare, but at least once or twice per day someone would harass me by giving me a hard stare or asking me what time it was, even though they were wearing a watch or looking at their cell phone. Having a camera in your hand will always cut back on any harassment—that cannot be said enough.

When I returned to North Carolina I would continue to have break-ins at my apartment and have clothing torn, ripped or punctured in exactly the same places.

In April of 2011, I moved back to Palm Springs, California. After about two weeks I became aware that the tile floor of my apartment would become increasingly scratched up, and there were new chips I would discover after going to the store. I began to hike and go mountain climbing again. There, it was just me and the mountain. Part of learning how to deal with the constant fear a Victim faces is forcing yourself to do things you used to do, and try to take back your life.

☙ Chapter Sixteen ❧

Today and the Future

"I remember the very things I do not wish to; I cannot forget the things I wish to forget."

Cicero

It is difficult to convey the life of a Targeted Individual. Every human being has their share of problems—health, financial, mental, and emotional. But the problem of being an ongoing Victim is completely in its own category— all by itself. A hard realization is the fact that we weep for no one but ourselves.

The reality of my situation, as with other Victims, is one of tolerance, not acceptance. I rarely try to convince non-Targets of the crime I endure every day. Even If I were to convince them, their belief is useless and does not change what is happening to me. For the first time that I am aware of, two days ago, I actually captured on my Sony Digital Voice Recorder someone breaking into my apartment on tape. One can hear the door opening and drawers being open and shut as well as a distinct grinding noise, as if someone was rubbing or damaging something intentionally. After a thorough and close inspection of my belongings, I noticed my brand new Arcteryx Bora 65 Backpack had unusual wear-and-tear on the back straps. I wear this back strap against my bare skin, so the now-existing damage could not have come from normal use.

Recently, I experienced corruption of food in my refrigerator. A chicken I had roasted was tainted with what I believe to be pure liquid Cocaine. One piece of chicken was extremely bitter; I could taste a chemical which left my lip and tongue numb for several hours. This is not uncommon, especially for Victims who have jobs which require random drug tests.

I have found that law enforcement likes to play the Devil's advocate, always quick to suggest anything except what I claim has happened to me or my property. It's like the old saying, "Police are always there when you don't need them, but they are never around when you do." My car continues to receive small scratches and minor vandalism.

All that any Victim can do is to try as best they can to ignore that which they anticipate and cannot change.

The future is unfortunate for current Victims and new Victims. The technology is smaller, faster, harder to detect, and nearly impossible to locate and remove or end its usage. Vitamins, exercise, a proper diet, and rest is really the only thing Targets can do for themselves. Precautions, such as motion activated cameras will nearly eliminate break-ins and further acts of vandalism; they, too, have their limitations. Placing a strong Neodymium magnet under one's chin and up against the throat will eliminate colored lights and swirling images that Targets typically experience when they close their eyes and try to sleep. Burns to the skin should be treated with antibiotic ointments several times daily to speed up healing and reduce scarring.

Although it is certainly easier said than done, keeping a sense of humor and enjoying as much as possible in this life, will inevitability help and distract the Victim from the constant fear of further harassment and torture. Never giving up hope is a must. Targets learn very quickly that a positive state of mind is their best friend. Every Target's situation is different, although there are certain similarities to others. Some Victims receive the constant 24/7 V2K (Voice to Skull) annoyance, others hear a constant ringing in the ears with tone bursts which cause them to wake up at night. Severe and unnatural pains to the heart, liver, and kidneys, and eye vision problems are all very common. New Victims, before they realize that they are, in fact, Targets, may misinterpret these symptoms as natural occurrences—but they are not. Torture, intimidation, and electronic harassment are all very real, not just in the minds of Targets, but in real life.

I am no different than any other Targeted Individual. I have, for the most part, gotten used to my life as a Victim. The more I give in to it and let it upset me—the more my criminals win. The more I am able to laugh, love, and live—the more I win.

Like everyone else, I want to live as long as I can and be as happy as I can be. I can actually say I am no longer afraid of dying—it's unavoidable, inevitable, and we can all count on it happening sooner or later.

My story is perhaps more unusual than some other Targets—not worse or better, but different. It seems every Victim I speak with always feels they have it worse than the next Victim—but they don't. Some are extremely, heavily Targeted, others receive a fraction of the harassment. Every Target—no matter how much intimidation and harassment that they are exposed to—is experiencing an amount which is too much. This crime should be stopped once and for all. The only way for this to be achieved is for Targets to revolt and stand up for themselves. My wish if for everyone to enjoy this journey called "life" and I hope and pray for a stop to this deep-rooted criminal behavior and torment. Most Targets are simply random Victims of a technology that is beyond comprehension.

Live and continue to love and somehow manage to smile through it all and you will find life worth living. This applies to everyone.

ᕫ Chapter Seventeen ᕬ

Overview: The Grand Royal Scam

"Man is the cruelest animal."

Friedrich Nietzsche

E veryone who hears my story always has the same question for me: *"Why would anyone want to do this to you? Can you imagine the tremendous financial cost and manpower resources needed to accomplish what you are explaining to me, and not get caught?"*

The master plan of this most elaborate and secretive of crimes involves three major components: World Domination, Depopulation, and Greed.

World Domination: Quite literally, total control of the entire planet. Control the market, control people's minds, their thoughts and dreams, and their health. This process also includes controlling things such as the weather, earthquakes, tsunamis, and "natural disasters." I recently spoke to a former C.I.A. agent, who shall remain anonymous. When I explained all that I knew about my situation he said he was familiar with the crime and even with all of my personal research. He said I have only scratched the surface with this book.

The broadcast news is completely sanitized, only revealing what people in lofty positions want the general public to know. If the world knew what the real news was, it would cause people to feel scared, betrayed, and angry—especially concerning matters involving the government and the military.

There are many thousands of Victims just like me who are heavily targeted, but there are many more that have been implanted and receive no harassment or intimidation. People who are being influenced or controlled without their realizing it can be referred to as "Sheeple," as they simply follow along, unaware of what is really already happening to them, their families, and friends.

Depopulation: Mankind is using up its resources faster than they can be replaced. Ultimately, when everything is depleted, we will simply cease to exist. In order to slow this process down, the governments of the world have devised a program to reduce the world's population. Slowly, almost at an infinitesimal pace, people are being "thinned out." Through medical conditions such as intentionally-induced cancer, heart attacks, and brain embolisms, people are living shorter lives in general. The very thought that this is happening as planned is disgusting and appalling to say the very least. To think our lives are being sped-up to further future generations is disturbing, unnatural, and immoral. How can I prove this? I have done enough research to know this is true; I don't have to prove it. Only human beings who are aware of the atrocities mankind commits against itself daily know this to be true. Proponents of the issue of chemtrails are a testament to my disclosures. Look up chemtrails; it is not just a conspiracy, it's a reality.

Greed: Of the seven deadly sins, greed is the most popular. It breeds and perpetuates itself. There is not much point in going into greater detail than greed for money, greed for domination, and greed for control of every living thing on this planet. Unfortunately, it is the starkest of truths.

Lastly, it's not too late; if people stop being "Sheeple" and wake up, things can and will change for the better. It really is sickening to realize our destinies are now being controlled against our nature, against our wills, even without our knowledge. I don't mean to be pessimistic or negative; I'm presenting things as they are. This presentation is, sadly, entirely true.

My story continues, as does my research. One voice can make a difference—it always does.

Closing Remarks

I relentlessly try to search for a surgeon or surgeons from all corners of the world to excise my foreign bodies. I refuse to give up hope.

The Invisible Crime - Michael F. Bell

There are only three possible reasons why every surgeon I have approached about removing any of my foreign objects refused to do so: either they are being paid off, they have been threatened not to remove them, or they are part of the conspiracy itself.

So, the story continues. . .

ᶜ⁄ᵉ Chapter Eighteen ᵉᵛᵒ

Patented Technology

"The future has been here for a long time."
Michael Fitzhugh Bell

The following is a complete list of declassified U.S. patents presently in use for mind control and electronic harassment in the United States and around the world:

Method of Changing a Person's Behavior: US Patent 4,717,34

A method of conditioning a person's unconscious mind in order to effect a desired change in the person's behavior which does not require the services of a trained therapist.

Subliminal Message Generator: US Patent 5,270,800

A combined subliminal and supraliminal message generator for use with a television receiver permits complete control of subliminal messages and their manner of presentation.

Method and System for Altering Consciousness: US Patent 5,123,899

A system for altering the states of human consciousness involves the simultaneous application of multi stimuli, preferable sounds, having differing frequencies and wave forms.

Hearing System: US Patent 4,877,027

Sound induced in the head of a person by radiating the head with microwaves in the range of 100 megahertz to 10,000 megahertz that are modulated with a particular waveform.

Communication System and Method Including Brain Wave Analysis and/or Use of Brain Activity: US Patent 6,011,991

A system and method for enabling human beings to communicate by way of their monitored brain activity.

Hearing Device: US Patent 4,858,612

A method and apparatus for stimulation of hearing in mammals by introduction of a plurality of microwaves into the region of the auditory cortex is shown and described.

Apparatus and Method for Remotely Monitoring and Altering Brainwaves: US Patent 3,951,134

Apparatus for and method of sensing brain waves at a position remote from a subject whereby electromagnetic signals of different frequencies are simultaneously transmitted to the brain of the subject in which the signals interfere with one another to yield a waveform which is modulated by the subjects brain waves.

Silent Subliminal Presentation System: US Patent 5,159,703

A silent communications system in which nonaural carriers, in the very low or very high audio frequency range or in the adjacent ultrasonic frequency spectrum, are amplitude or frequency modulated with the desired intelligence and propagated acoustically or vibrationally, for inducement into the brain, typically through the use of loudspeakers, earphones or piezoelectric transducers.

Method and an Associated Apparatus for Remotely Determining Information as to a Person's Emotional State: US Patent 5,507,291

Implantable Transceiver: US Patent US5629678

Apparatus for tracking and recovering humans.

Barcode Tattoo: US Patent 5,878,155

Method for verifying human identity during electronic sale transactions.

Ultrasonic Speech Translator and Communications System.: US Patent 5,539,705

A wireless communication system undetectable by radio frequency methods for converting audio signals, including human voice, to electronic signals in the ultrasonic frequency range, transmitting the ultrasonic signal by way of acoustical pressure across the carrier medium, including gases, liquids, or solids, and reconverting the ultrasonic acoustical pressure waves back to the original audio signal.

Personal Tracking and Recovery System: US Patent 5,629,678

Apparatus for tracking and recovering humans utilizes an implantable transceiver incorporating a power supply and actuation system allowing the unit to remain implanted and functional for years without maintenance.

Intra-Oral Tracking Device: US Patent 5,760,692

An intra-oral tracking device adapted for use in association with a tooth having a buccal surface and a lingual surface, the apparatus comprises a tooth mounting member having an inner surface and an outer surface, the inner surface including adhesive material.

Fenceless Animal Control System Using GPS Location Information: US Patent 5,868,100

A fenceless animal confinement system comprising of portable units attached to the animal and including means for receiving GPS signals and for providing stimulation to the animal.

Global Position Satellite Tracking Device: US Patent 5,905,461

A global positioning and tracking system for locating one of a person and item of property.

Magnetic Excitation of Sensory Resonance: US Patent 5,935,05

The invention pertains to influencing the nervous system of a subject by a weak externally applied magnetic field with a frequency near 1/2 Hz. In a range of amplitudes, such fields can excite the 1/2 sensory resonance, which is the psychological effect involved in "rocking the baby."

Engine Disabling Weapon: US Patent 5,952,600

A non-lethal weapon for disabling an engine such as that of a fleeing car by means of a high voltage discharge that perturbs or destroys the electrical circuits.

Speech Signal Processing for Determining Psychological or Physiological Characteristics Using a Knowledge Base: US Patent 6,006,188

Body Worn Active and Passive Tracking Device. US Patent 6,014,080. Tamper resistant body-worn tracking device to be worn by offenders or potential Victims for use in wireless communication system receiving signals from a global positioning system (GPS).

Subliminal Acoustic Manipulation of Nervous System: US Patent 6,017,302

In human subjects, sensory resonance can be excited by subliminal atmospheric acoustic pulses that are tuned to the resonance frequency.

Methods and Formulations for Modulating the Human Sexual Response: US Patent 6,051,594

190

The Invisible Crime - Michael F. Bell

The invention is directed to improved methods for modulating the human sexual response by orally administering a formulation of the vasodilator phentolamine to the blood circulation and thereby modulating the sexual response on demand.

Apparatus and Method of Broadcasting Audible Sound Using Ultrasonic Sound as a Carrier: US Patent 6,052,336

An ultrasonic sound source broadcasts an ultrasonic signal which is amplitude and/or frequency modulated with an information input signal originating from an information input source.

Katz, Bruce. Method and Device for Producing a Desired Brain State: US Patent 6,488,617 (December 3, 2002)

A method and device for the production of a desired brain state in an individual contain means for monitoring and analyzing the brain state while a set of one or more magnets produce fields that alter this state. A computational system alters various parameters of the magnetic fields in order to close the gap between the actual and desired brain state. This feedback process operates continuously until the gap is minimized and/or removed.

Tosaya, Caro: Signal Injection Coupling into the Human Vocal Trac:. US Patent 6,487,531 (November 26, 2002)

A means and method are provided for enhancing or replacing the natural excitation of the human vocal tract by artificial excitation means, wherein the artificially created acoustics present additional spectral, temporal, or phase data useful for (1) enhancing the machine recognition robustness of audible speech or (2) enabling more robust machine-recognition of relatively inaudible mouthed or whispered speech. The artificial excitation (a) may be arranged to be audible or inaudible, (b) may be designed to be non-interfering with another user's similar means, (c) may be used in one or both of a vocal content-enhancement mode or a complimentary vocal tract-probing mode, and/or (d) may be used for the recognition of audible or inaudible continuous speech or isolated spoken commands.

Karell, Manuel. Method and Apparatus for Treating Auditory Hallucinations: US Patent 6,430,443. (August 6, 2002)

Stimulating one or more vestibulocochlear nerves or cochlea or cochlear regions will treat, prevent and control auditory hallucinations.

Gerosa, William. Portable and Hand-Held Device for Making Humanly Audible Sounds: US Patent 6,426,919. (July 30, 2002)

A portable and hand-held device for making humanly audible sounds responsive to the detecting of ultrasonic sounds. The device includes a hand-held housing and circuitry that is contained in the housing. The circuitry includes a microphone that receives the ultrasonic sound, a first low voltage audio power amplifier that strengthens the signal from the microphone, a second low voltage audio power amplifier that further strengthens the signal from the first low voltage audio power amplifier, a 7-stage ripple carry binary counter that lowers the frequency of the signal from the second low voltage audio power amplifier so as to be humanly audible, a third low voltage audio power amplifier that strengthens the signal from the 7-stage ripple carry binary counter, and a speaker that generates a humanly audible sound from the third low voltage audio power amplifier.

Patton, Richard. Method and Apparatus for Analyzing Neurological Response to Emotion-Inducing Stimuli: US Patent 6,292,688. (September 18, 2001)

A method of determining the extent of the emotional response of a test subject to stimuli having a time-varying visual content, for example, an advertising presentation. The test subject is positioned to observe the presentation for a given duration, and a path of communication is established between the subject and a brain wave detector/analyzer. The intensity component of each of at least two different brain wave frequencies is measured during the exposure, and each frequency is associated with a particular emotion. While the subject views the presentation, periodic variations in the intensity component of the brain waves of each of the particular frequencies selected is measured. The change rates in the intensity at regular periods during the duration are also measured. The intensity change rates are then used to construct a graph of plural coordinate points, and these coordinate points graphically establish the composite emotional reaction of the subject as the presentation continues.

Rose, John. Behavior Modification: US Patent 6,258,022 (July 10,2001)

Behavior modification of a human subject takes place

under hypnosis, when the subject is in a relaxed state. A machine plays back a video or audio recording, during which the subject is instructed to activate a device to create a perceptible stimulation which is linked, through the hypnosis, with a visualization of enhanced or improved performance. After the hypnosis, the user can reactivate the device at will, whenever the improved performance, such as an improved sporting performance, is desired. This will again create the perceptible stimulation and thus induce the required visualization.

Glen, Jeffrey. Intra-Oral Electronic Tracking Device: US Patent 6,239,705 (May 29,2001)

An improved stealthy, non-surgical, biocompatible electronic tracking device is provided in which a housing is placed intraorally. The housing contains micro circuitry. The micro circuitry comprises a receiver, a passive mode to active mode activator, a signal decoder for determining positional fix, a transmitter, an antenna, and a power supply. Optionally, an amplifier may be utilized to boost signal strength. The power supply energizes the receiver. Upon receiving a coded activating signal, the positional fix signal decoder is energized, determining a positional fix. The transmitter subsequently transmits through the antenna a position locating signal to be received by a remote locator. In another embodiment of the present invention, the micro circuitry comprises a receiver, a passive mode to active mode activator, a transmitter, an antenna and a power supply. Optionally, an amplifier may be utilized to boost signal strength. The power supply energizes the receiver. Upon receiving a coded activating

194

signal, the transmitter is energized. The transmitter subsequently transmits through the antenna a homing signal to be received by a remote locator.

Loos, Hendricus. Pulse Variability in Electric Field Manipulation of Nervous Systems: US Patent 6,167,304 (December 26, 2000)

Apparatus and method for manipulating the nervous system of a subject by applying to the skin a pulsing external electric field which, although too weak to cause classical nerve stimulation, modulates the normal spontaneous spiking patterns of certain kinds of afferent nerves. For certain pulse frequencies the electric field stimulation can excite in the nervous system resonances with observable physiological consequences. Pulse variability is introduced for the purpose of thwarting habituation of the nervous system to the repetitive stimulation, or to alleviate the need for precise tuning to a resonance frequency, or to control pathological oscillatory neural activities such as tremors or seizures. Pulse generators with stochastic and deterministic pulse variability are disclosed, and the output of an effective generator of the latter type is characterized.

Bowman, Gerard D., et al. Method of Inducing Harmonious States of Being: US Patent 6,135,94. (October 24, 2000)

A method of inducing harmonious states of being using vibrational stimuli, preferably sound, comprised of a multitude of frequencies expressing a specific pattern of relationship. Two base signals are modulated by a set of ratios to generate a plurality of harmonics. The harmonics are combined to form a "fractal" arrangement.

Jandel, Magnus. Subliminal Message Protection: US Patent 6,122,322 (September 19, 2000)

The present invention relates to a method and to a system for detecting a first context change between two frames. When a second context change between a further two frames occurs within a predetermined time interval, the frames accommodated within the two context changes are defined as a subliminal message. An alarm is sent to an observer upon detection of a subliminal message.

Loos, Hendricus. Pulsative Manipulation of Nervous Systems: US Patent 6,091,994 (July 18, 2000)

Method and apparatus for manipulating the nervous system by imparting subliminal pulsative cooling to the subject's skin at a frequency that is suitable for the excitation of a sensory resonance. At present, two major sensory resonances are known, with frequencies near 1/2 Hz and 2.4 Hz. The 1/2 Hz sensory resonance causes relaxation, sleepiness, ptosis of the eyelids, a tonic smile, a "knot" in the stomach, or sexual excitement, depending on the precise frequency used. The 2.4 Hz resonance causes the slowing of certain cortical activities, and is characterized by a large increase of the time needed to silently count backward from 100 to 60, with the eyes closed. The invention can be used by the general public for inducing relaxation, sleep, or sexual excitement, and clinically for the control and perhaps a treatment of tremors, seizures, and autonomic system disorders such as panic attacks. Embodiments shown are a pulsed fan to impart subliminal cooling pulses to the subject's skin, and a silent device which induces periodically varying flow past the subject's skin, the flow being induced by pulsative rising warm air plumes that are caused by a thin resistive wire which is periodically heated by electric current pulses.

Loos, Hendricus. Electric Fringe Field Generator for Manipulating Nervous Systems: US Patent 6,081,744 (June 27, 2000)

Apparatus and method for manipulating the nervous system of a subject through afferent nerves, modulated by externally applied weak fluctuating electric fields, tuned to certain frequencies such as to excite a resonance in neural circuits. Depending on the frequency chosen, excitation of such resonances causes in a human subject relaxation, sleepiness, sexual excitement, or the slowing of certain cortical processes. The electric field used for stimulation of the subject is induced by a pair of field electrodes charged to opposite polarity and placed such that the subject is entirely outside the space between the field electrodes. Such configuration allows for very compact devices where the field electrodes and a battery-powered voltage generator are contained in a small casing, such as a powder box. The stimulation by the weak external electric field relies on frequency modulation of spontaneous spiking patterns of afferent nerves. The method and apparatus can be used by the general public as an aid to relaxation, sleep, or arousal, and clinically for the control and perhaps the treatment of tremors and seizures, and disorders of the autonomic nervous system, such as panic attacks.

Lowrey, Austin, III. Apparatus and Method of Broadcasting Audible Sound Using Ultrasonic Sound as a Carrier US Patent 6,052,336 (April 18, 2000)

An ultrasonic sound source broadcasts an ultrasonic signal which is amplitude and/or frequency modulated with an information input signal originating from an information input source. If the signals are amplitude modulated, a square root function of the information input signal is produced prior to modulation. The modulated signal, which may be amplified, is then broadcast via a projector unit, whereupon an individual or group of individuals located in the broadcast region detect the audible sound.

Douglas, Peter, et al. Therapeutic Behavior Modification Program, Compliance Monitoring and Feedback System US Patent 6,039,688 (March 21, 2000)

A therapeutic behavior modification program, compliance monitoring and feedback system includes a server-based relational database and one or more microprocessors electronically coupled to the server. The system enables development of a therapeutic behavior modification program having a series of milestones for an individual to achieve lifestyle changes necessary to maintain his or her health or recover from ailments or medical procedures. The program may be modified by a physician or trained case advisor prior to implementation. The system monitors the individual's compliance with the program by prompting the individual to enter health-related data, correlating the individual's entered data with the milestones in the behavior modification program and generating compliance data indicative of the individual's progress toward achievement of the program milestones. The system also includes an integrated system of graphical system interfaces for motivating the individual to comply with the program. Through the interfaces, the individual can access the database to review the compliance data and obtain health information from a remote source such as selected sites on the Internet. The system also provides an electronic calendar integrated with the behavior modification program for signaling the individual to take action pursuant to the behavior modification program in which the calendar accesses the relational database and integrates requirements of the program with the individual's daily schedule, and an electronic journal for enabling the individual to enter personal health-related information into the system on a regular basis. In addition, the system includes an electronic meeting room for linking the individual to a plurality of other individuals having related behavior modification programs for facilitating group peer support sessions for compliance with the program. The system enables motivational media presentations to be made to the individuals in the electronic meeting room as part of the group support session to facilitate interactive group discussion about the presentations. The entire system is designed around a community of support motif including a graphical electronic navigator operable by the individual to control the microprocessor for accessing different parts of the system.

*Loos, Hendricus. **Subliminal Acoustic Manipulation of Nervous Systems: US Patent 6,017,30. (January 25, 2000)***

In human subjects, sensory resonances can be excited by subliminal atmospheric acoustic pulses that are tuned to the resonance frequency. The 1/2 Hz sensory resonance affects the autonomic nervous system and may cause relaxation, drowsiness, or sexual excitement, depending on the precise acoustic frequency near 1/2 Hz used. The effects of the 2.5 Hz resonance include slowing of certain cortical processes, sleepiness, and disorientation. For these effects to occur, the acoustic intensity must lie in a certain deeply subliminal range. Suitable apparatus consists of a portable battery-powered source of weak sub-audio acoustic radiation. The method and apparatus can be used by the general public as an aid to relaxation, sleep, or sexual arousal, and clinically for the control and perhaps treatment of insomnia, tremors, epileptic seizures, and anxiety disorders. There is further application as a nonlethal weapon that can be used in law enforcement standoff situations, for causing drowsiness and disorientation in Targeted subjects. It is then preferable to use venting acoustic monopoles in the form of a device that inhales and exhales air with sub-audio frequency.

THE END

❧ References ❧

John Mecca and his website: www.us-government-torture.com

My friend and author, Dr. John Hall and his book, *A New Breed – Satellite Terrorism in America.* His website: www.satweapons.com

Dr. Anna Fubini and her website: http://www.aisjca-mft.org/chips-viol.htm

John Flemming, July 14th, 2001. *The Shocking Menace of Satellite Surveillance*, Pravda, RU.

Special thanks to my loyal friends and fellow Targeted Individuals:

Enrique "Henry" Garay Perez

Roger Tolces

Blanche Chavoustie

Eleanor White

Marcia Lee

Dwight Mangum

Dr. John Hall.

Without the support and friendship of these people, my life would have been much worse.

ᓚ About Michael F. Bell ᓫ

Michael Fitzhugh Bell is a graduate of the Culinary Institute of America. He is a classically trained chef who has worked in Hotels in Austria and has worked in some very well-known restaurants and hotels in America. He spent several years working in the entertainment business in Hollywood, California, as a motion picture catering chef and aspiring screenwriter. He also trains for and does high-altitude mountaineering, climbing big peaks around the world.

Michael has written articles for Palm Springs Life magazine and won several writing contests while at prep school and college. This book was written after seven years of exhausting research. Michael is considered a Targeted Individual. This book was written for two reasons: to make the American public aware of this technology and the unconscionable crimes for which it is used, and to help other Targeted Individuals gain control of their lives and cope with this nightmare from which they never seem to wake.

CPSIA information can be obtained
at www.ICGtesting.com
Printed in the USA
BVHW09s1752150718
521676BV00008B/111/P